The Ten Minute Moment

A week long adventure in Consciousness

Jurgen Ziewe

ISBN 978-1-291-60306-4

Copyright © 2013 by Jurgen Ziewe

The right of Jurgen Ziewe to be identified as the author of the work
has been asserted by him in accordance with the Copyright,
Design and Patents Act 1988. All rights reserved.
The copyright act prohibits the making of copies of this work
or of a substantial part of it. This includes making copies
via photocopying or similar process via electronic means.
Edited by Ian Allan

This book is dedicated
to all who are seeking
Liberation, Fulfilment and Enlightenment

With special thanks to Dhanakosa,
who made this most memorable
experience possible

The Retreat	1
Day one, Friday 31 May Arrival	6
Day two, Saturday 1 June Dreams and Meditation	14
Day three, Sunday 2 June Illusion and Reality	37
Day four, Monday 3 June The Alternative Life	60
Day five, Tuesday 4 June The Terrifying Face of God	79
Day six, Wednesday 5 June The Ten Minute Moment	106
Day seven, Thursday, 6 June Translocating Identity	125

The Retreat

Some people regard exposing the most intimate aspect of their inner lives as a great taboo, and what could be more private than laying bare that part which defines us as individuals and human beings? I have spoken to other people who have had similar experiences to mine, which I am about to lay open, who were adamant that such revelation would compromise and even destroy the most precious and sacred quality within them. I disagree. I feel it is my duty to report it as faithfully as possible and lay open the most sacred parts of my soul, because I now know that at the very root of it all is the one attribute we all have in common and which defines us as a divine species. Having witnessed it I feel obliged to report, to instil confidence in others, to grasp and acknowledge this innermost truth. Not doing so would be negligent at a time when so much confusion rules and ruins so many aspects of our existence.

Time has long moved on since I had one of the most powerful experiences in consciousness of my entire life and it has left me viewing the world from a unique and new perspective. To use a metaphor, it was an experience that has taken me from the cellar to the top of an infinite roof garden, from which I can enjoy the bright sunlight and a magnificent view of the world around me. As I am typing out my notes I am still on my roof garden, despite having re-entered my old life dressed in the same old body, executing its old roles. How long I will remain here, I cannot tell; I guess as long as I allow life to renew itself on a moment-by-moment basis I may remain here forever, but who is to say.

For the time being my new life is here, now, and on this new level, stripped of its old history. Every new moment gives me the opportunity to start my life afresh, reaching into a new overlay of clarity which is only an attention away and transcends all thoughts of yesterday. For now my actions are carried by an inner stillness. Thoughts, which don't demand my immediate attention are little more than messages in a bottle, seen from the deck of an ocean liner. They no longer have the significance or importance they once commanded and instead intuitive thinking has taken their place, thinking which rises out of a deep inner stillness via the heart, concerning itself with what is true and authentic. The commentator who had been squatting inside my head has retired, his cold judgements laid to rest; instead I bask in the unlimited freedom of a new stillness which rises from my heart and is offering me with renewed insistence every moment as a potential for joy. That's why my days begin with gratitude. How can they not? And what else is gratitude than the doorway for love?

The Ten Minute Moment

These are the journals of a week in retreat, a true story, a step-by-step account of my experiences where I surrendered thought in order to focus attention on reality, moment by moment, without being restricted by expectations or judgement. I had granted myself the freedom to ignore time and all its commitments. I had no telephone, no internet, no way of communicating with the outside world. Instead I made a silent vow to surrender my complete attention to that which simply is, to a state of being which is unpolluted by personal issues, the world's obligations and concerns. Yet were they to arise I was eager to view them like any other aspect of my external reality: without judgement, without involvement or attachment. I had entered a state of constant meditation and stillness. I was there to find out what reality was made of without the filters of personal desires and obsessions. In the end it culminated in a ten-minute moment that elevated my life.

The place I had chosen for focusing attention was a remote log cabin up in the Scottish mountains, hidden from human eyes, tucked away and off the beaten track. There were no paths leading to it, because there was no traffic. It was maintained by a small community of Buddhist devotees, almost keeping it a secret. It was a Westerner's equivalent of a Sadhu's cave.

The moment I turned the car into the single-track lane leading to my retreat it already felt good. The long journey, which I had leisurely scheduled over two days, stopping off for one night at a hotel in the Lake District, had come to its end. At the entrance of the road stood a young woman hitching a lift. I felt thrilled that I was greeted with an opportunity to help somebody's progress. The hitchhiker was in her early twenties. She told me that she was a student on work placement, employed at a hotel a fair distance up the long, winding road. When she asked where I was heading I told her about the monastery and my solitary retreat. She knew the place and even knew how to pronounce it correctly.

After driving for just a few hundred yards I was charmed by the splendour of the scenery. A loch was to the left and a mountain gradually grew in size to our right as we drove along, increasingly squeezing our narrow lane towards the lake.

'Where are you from?' I asked her, curious about her strong foreign accent.

'I am from Lithuania,' she replied, then added, 'You can drop me off at your retreat. I am used to walking. It will only be another two miles from there.'

I felt disappointment that she was threatening to cut my journey short as I drank in thirstily the breathtaking scenery which was unravelling with every new bend of the road.

'Oh please,' I insisted, 'I don't mind at all dropping you off a little bit further.'

Naturally there was no argument and the decision showed synchronicity because whenever we encountered oncoming traffic after we passed the point where my retreat was signposted, it always happened at a rare spot wide enough for two passing cars.

The scenery became more enchanting at every turn: a bridge with a stream here, fallen trees covered in moss to the left, a clear view of the lake with a giant rock jutting majestically into the air after another bend. To our right languished a great mountain, stripped of all trees and seamed by raw granite outcrops. I was grateful that the potholed road forced my speed down and gave me an excuse to keep one eye glued to the scenery, while the other eye reluctantly scanned for holes in the road. Eventually we clattered over a cattle grid and stopped at her hotel.

Day one, Friday 31 May
Arrival

After unloading my passenger I traced my journey back to the retreat. At the gate to the main admin building I was greeted by a solemn-looking angel, a young girl in her twenties, wearing a long flowing dress and who appeared to be leaving just as I arrived. She offered to open the gate, which looked far too heavy for her elf-like stature, and with a grateful nod I drove through and parked the car.

The Buddhist community, where I was meant to pick up the keys for my solitary home, consisted of a series of whitewashed buildings. They lay there peacefully, looking unoccupied yet not quite deserted. Calmness was imprinted on it. I looked out for any signs of residents but there were none. I entered the main door to the first building, but it seemed deserted. Skirting the outside in an

1 – The Nine-Step Meditation towards Awakening

LOVE

This is a nine-part meditation technique like no other. It relies on an attitude of passive attention, which means rather than me meditating I am meditated. It also implies a surrender to this process of 'being meditated'. The power of this technique lies in the intent being placed in the stillness surrounding me or surrendering to it rather than coming from me. This is a very subtle distinction, but very powerful.

My first meditation is LOVE. I don't think about love or how it relates to me. I simply find the 'feeling tone' of love, love itself. This and all the following meditations are based on finding the 'feeling tone', noticing that LOVE is a manifestation and attribute of the clear light of consciousness, an outpouring of it which does not come from me but from a higher source. I find the feeling tone of love until I experience it directly and then I let it go, allow it out into the universe. I surrender to it and let it unfold. One minute, or even seconds, are enough, because the power of love is much greater when I don't interfere but simply surrender myself to it. I don't contemplate or think about love. I just gently allow it to take me with it.

obvious lost manner I was hoping to be caught, but wasn't. The second building showed more signs of occupation, cloths neatly hung up on hangers on the wall. In another room I saw tastefully displayed Buddhist merchandise, little statues, incense and an arrangement of highly artistic photographs of the surrounding area, but sadly no one to greet me.

Finally the friendly face of a young woman showed up and directed me to the office. I was introduced to the leader of the community for the formalities, then was sent straight to a larder room which was stacked high with provisions. Here I was invited to help myself to a week's supply of food. Being handed a 'Bag for Life' with the logo of a large supermarket chain emboldened on it, I went 'shopping'. Unprepared, I scoured the baskets of fresh vegetables and fruit and without plans or strategy I grabbed two onions, five potatoes, two leeks, four tomatoes, one courgette and one red pepper. Looking slightly lost I asked my assisting host if they provided bread as well. He opened a large freezer and pulled out a frozen loaf of brown bread and a bulging two-litre bottle of milk, yellowed into a frozen block of ice. There were other things on offer, such as garlic, fruit and nuts, but no recipe for such ingredients sprang to mind and I called it a day.

Next my host offered to take my heavy suitcase, which also contained all my camera equipment and my mouldable bean chair, which I had especially purchased solely for reasons of comfort. He strapped everything on his quad bike, rolled up the hill and disappeared into the thickets.

There was only room for one on his bike and so I had to walk. I struggled to keep up by memorising the features of the bushes he had disappeared into but then he vanished completely with barely a visible track left. I pricked my ears to trace the direction of the thinning sound and then I followed, mostly using instinct and the giveaway signs of flattened grass made by two tyre tracks. Scrambling up a steep hill I finally caught up. My Buddhist friend was already unloading the luggage at the refuge hut. I was still out of breath and unable to speak, and he received me with a wry grin and led me into the cabin.

The Sheilin, as the wooden hut is known to the community of buddhists, was about eight feet deep by twelve feet long. In the corner was a bed and opposite a desk and chair. At the other side was the 'kitchen', a small corner unit with a microwave-sized oven on top featuring two electric rings. Further along, under the window, was the sink with draining board and a small extra worktop. Above and below were storage units. In the middle of the hut was a little altar with a Buddha statue carved out of wood, two large and several smaller candles surrounding it. There were ample supplies of incense and lighters right next to the place of worship as well as a Buddhist prayer book. In front of the altar was the mat with the meditation seat and to the left of it were carefully folded blankets and seating cushions. In the corner, leaning against the ensuite shower room and toilet, was a small armchair with worn-out cushions.

My guide grabbed a first-aid kit which was in a basket next to the kitchen unit.

'Just in case,' he smiled. 'There are no ambulances out here, but here is everything you need in case of an emergency.' Without me paying too much attention he talked about wound dressings, disinfectants and then explained to me with a more serious expression that sometimes sheep ticks would bury themselves under the skin and that it would be advisable to familiarise myself with the tweezers, shrink-wrapped in sterile sealers. He explained their use and how to pull out ticks which lived in the long grass and were active at this time of year. He also explained to me the use of disinfectant as a first line of defence and that in some cases a negligent attitude could result in Lyme disease, which could cripple me for the rest of my life.

I thanked him for his advice and after he had drawn my attention to all amenities I complimented him on the unexpected five-star service and the simple luxury of my accommodation. With monk-like indifference to my flattery he smiled and retreated.

After about an hour of settling in I made tea in true English fashion. The frozen milk yielded just enough defrosted liquid for one cup. I moved my beanbag in front of the open door where for the first time I relished a view which literally exceeded all my expectations, and my ears began to feast on a quietness they had not experienced for a long time, but within half an hour I had nodded off.

For my supper I had a banana and an orange I had brought with me, in contrast to the burger I had consumed at the motorway service station earlier in the day, but it was just enough. I also had a cup of green tea and a low-calorie biscuit, which my dear wife had lovingly added to my provisions for the journey. The position of my bean chair was now ordained as my main spot in the Sheilin from where I would conduct all my meditation and hopefully my excursions into the higher states of consciousness. With that in mind I gave it a trial run, my first evening meditation.

This was a mixture of tiredness, sleep and half-hearted attempts at focusing my attention on stillness, a stillness broken only by the fluttering noise of wings and chirping of birds which congregated outside my door. A thoughtful member of the community had placed a bird feeder for entertainment. Tiredness prevailed and I decided to call it a day. I closed the door for the night. In vain I looked for means of locking it. The only extra security was provided by a heavy curtain which I pulled across it. It's strange how conditioned we are into locking our doors for the night and how insecure we feel when these measures are taken away from us. I decided to go to bed.

1st of June 2013, first night

It was extremely cold, not like the comfortable home I was used to. I was glad to have brought my track suit for comfort, which I decided to wear over my pyjamas. I never pretended to be an Indian Sadhu who could live a life of deprivation in a cave in order to attain enlightenment. I am just a regular guy of pensionable age, spoilt by the comforts of modern living, so deciding to go for extra warmth caused no moral dilemma. I briefly reflected back on my youth and the last time I had lived in the wild when camping out with friends, but then I was not even alone. Here, in my log cabin, I was not even in shouting distance from the nearest house which in turn was miles away from the nearest village. Yet I liked it, it worked both ways. I was inaccessible, no phone, no contact and few chances of being discovered or disturbed accidentally. By the time I was ready for bed nature outside my cabin had already gone to sleep. The peace was incredible.

I drew all the blinds in front of the window. The closed curtain in front of the door at least it gave me the illusion that I was safe. The pillows on my bed were two compressed lumps, flat and unyielding. I found my anticipation proven right. They were much too uncomfortable and with a sense of satisfaction I replaced them with two brand new pillows I had brought with me as a precaution. The quality of my sleep always heavily depended on the softness of my pillow. Thus prepared I had no problems dropping off to sleep as the long journey had taken its toll.

Day two, Saturday 1 June
Dreams and Meditation

I woke up at 5 a.m. I hadn't slept very well at all. Not being used to such isolation, subconsciously part of me may have been on the lookout motivated by irrational security concerns, in case some mythical troll or a Scottish mountain spirit stumbled across my isolated abode and forced its entry through the unlockable door. Realistically they had a bigger chance of disturbing my sleep than any human strangers. It's weird how our conditioning forces us to lock ourselves in and secure the windows every night in our urban areas without even thinking about it, programmed to anticipate danger. The only thing out here disturbing my sleep would most likely be nothing more than the scratching of tiny feet outside the door or the occasional noise of harmless nocturnal creatures. Now awake, I opened the blinds and drew the curtain at the door to let in the predawn light. The sun had not yet risen and it would take some time for its golden globe to appear over the mountain, but a deer was already grazing just fifty yards away and it only gave me a casual glance looking up as I opened the door to let in the fresh morning air. I grabbed my camera and took my first picture of wildlife.

However, despite the fragmented night, I'd had dreams which still lingered in my memory and which appeared significant.

In this dream I was in a house which was in a state of renovation and extension. A few workmen were busy with their jobs. Raw wooden joists were exposed on the floor and a pile of pink, drying clay or cement was carelessly heaped right in the middle of the room. I pointed this out to one of the workers and asked why it was taking so long to finish my building. He simply shrugged his shoulders and carried on. I then wanted to know where the project manager was but was simply told that he had left; I let everyone just get on with their work.

I went on to inspect the rest of my house. I came across three or four workmen busying themselves with various tasks, but it was all uncoordinated and the whole place was in a mess. I turned to one guy who I identified as Andy. Andy seemed to be pregnant with a large protruding belly. I asked him whether he would be willing to take over as project manager to complete the house and then I whinged on about how if we didn't pull together and complete it the whole build would simply bankrupt me. Andy couldn't care less. 'Not my job,' he said.

Even as I was dreaming this I pondered the significance and clearly drew a parallel between the house and my own personal development. Dreams are a dead giveaway about our psychological and spiritual state. I concluded that Andy, the 'pregnant' worker I had tried to assign responsibility to, was me, pregnant with good intentions, just needing a push to complete the house of my whole self, renovated from the ground up, ready for a new beginning, but it was up to me to put everything into action to complete the process.

Often my dreams are semi-lucid, where I start the dream interpretation while still in a dream. I always thought this to be the by-product of meditation, which has taught me to become more aware, with this awareness spilling over into my dream life.

The Ten Minute Moment

I had accepted a long time ago that we use our dreams to perform actual tasks which relate to our waking life reality. When being confronted with problems or issues of other people, I often found myself dealing with their issue in the dream state, discussing their problems, helping them to look at life more positively. Occasionally I noticed when dreaming about friends and discussing their issues in the dream state that later their problem was of lesser significance or even was resolved altogether.

Later on, I had another dream. This time it was even more lucid, and took place in a small room with two other guys. I found out that they were from Istanbul. I didn't trust them. They were plotting something which I could tell by instinct and without doubt. My dream painted them as fanatical Islamist types, almost a caricature, the way they are often portrayed on wanted posters. Their inscrutable demeanour didn't help to dispel my suspicion. For some unknown reason I felt obliged to enter a discussion with them about tolerance, which was clearly not appreciated. They told me that they couldn't give a hoot about me or what I thought and that I should mind my own business. By then I could clearly intuit that they were hatching a plan involving a terror plot and at this point I felt it was my duty to intervene by reminding them that the core of their religion was love, as was the core with all religions, and remembering that would allow them to negotiate their lives more effectively, build bridges to other people and serve their religion best. All this was wasted effort and all I received back were threatening glances.

I simply filed these episodes away as a dream encounter which may or may not have had any relationship to reality. If it did I may have simply picked up my own thoughts or the ideas of other people. I decided to discard all this and instead turned to meditation.

It was chilly. I could clearly feel the change in altitude and I decided to put on an extra jumper, then settled down for my first meditation. I had the door wide open and overlooked a pastoral landscape: over grass, through the trees and on to the mountain opposite beyond the lake.

Meditation, 5:30 a.m.

Focusing on the light in my meditation appeals to my visually biased nature as an artist. I feel that once the art of focusing attention has been mastered, meditation is a dynamic process like the organic flow of energy itself shaping all nature. I am nature and meditation for me is a natural process.

My thoughts too are nature and leaving them to their own devices allows them to control and dominate my life. To put myself in charge I have learned to focus my attention. A long time ago I discovered simple methods which taught me to give preference to my intent. I found that my brain could be trained like a dog. I did that by gently and persistently reminding it to favour the meditation rather than my thoughts and I rewarded it with love. Eventually it became like a well-trodden path, similar to finding my way through high grass to get to my cottage in the middle of a field. If I keep changing my path I'll always have to keep treading the grass down again, which is laborious, and when I return to the previous path the grass will have already overgrown my path, so I'll have to start again. So I keep it simple for my brain by reminding it to favour the meditation, thus keeping the path to my cottage clear.

There are of course many ways and methods and many teachers, but this is my way. I can focus on whatever I choose and when thoughts arise I simply take note and then allow my attention to return to my intent and I find little rebellion. This gentle and persistent decision making has trained my brain to follow my intent and not my thoughts. Another way to master my thoughts is simply by residing in an emotional state of gratitude and love. This is a natural and very rewarding way to hold attention and find my way into stillness. Now it takes only minutes to get into a deep state. In the end consciousness picks up and does the meditation for me.

An important aspect for me is to remember that during meditation I am not trying to get anywhere, but that I am already here and wherever I am is perfect for me because stillness is already here. And it is not dependent on what I think or where I am. So if I intend to focus on the light, for example, I don't see the light as something to focus on which is separate, but experience that I am the light already. So there is nothing I need to attain.

Meditation to me is a dynamic process. It takes into account all kinds of things that may happen during the process, but never am I trying to get anywhere or achieve anything as it is not about making progress or getting anywhere, meditation is about waking up and becoming aware of what is and what moves it. And what is, is that I am the thought or the event that happens to be, I am the breath I breathe, the light I see, the mantra I pick. I am what is. I am and have been unified consciousness all along and all I need to focus on is to keep being it. This is my meditation, it is absolute freedom. Whatever I choose to focus my attention on and what I choose to be, I will become.

This time I perceived light as an illuminated space above the crown of my head or perhaps just inside the top of my skull. Instead of seeing myself separated from it, I imagined taking residence in that space and merging with the light rather than visualising it. After all, what or who am I? Who I am is only built on assumptions accumulated over the course of my life, something which is totally nonspecific and vague. Why not strip it down to its core axiom: awareness? And if I cannot grasp such abstract concept as awareness, why not give it more materiality and see it as light, the axiom for all life, the core energy for existence. This way I can directly relate to it like I can relate to my body.

Focusing on the light, it didn't take too long before I had a powerful sense of being just that, a light at the core of my being of which I knew it was the closest reflection of reality, closer even than feeling my body. At the same time thoughts became more sparse and soon were dispelled quickly; so were the scenes which emerged from the thoughts.

Then, without warning and out of nowhere, I became aware of a number of human characters parading in front of my inner vision. This is quite a common feature in meditation when personal thinking takes second place. The mind is eager to grab hold of new information and turns into a radio receiver for input. It may catch some fragments of conversation people may be having elsewhere, which are broadcast and now received by the radio antenna within my brain. How little we know about our brains and its complex set of skills which we only now are just beginning to understand. This new input is authentic. It can be pieces of conversation by individuals almost anywhere in the world which the brain grabs hold of, ranging from people discussing business to a couple arguing, to any other trivial scene of everyday life that could be happening anywhere in the world outside. We are even able to pick up the emotion, tone of voice and the personality of the individuals broadcasting.

This was just another distraction, however, and only served to remind me what an incredible organ the brain is. So the first thing I did was to switch off the channel, but almost as soon as I tuned out another programme was dialled up. I became the receiving station for a number of human characters who started appearing in front of my mind's eye, but now they were visual, more than just sound bites. They were fully three-dimensional and in full colour, a result of the fact that I had tuned into a higher frequency. I was now privy to studying a number of strange yet very real characters from a more perceptive point of view and a higher perspective. I had also moved to the point of perceiving people more authentically, which revealed their appearance as costumes, perhaps shells or superficial dressings. All of the characters parading in front of me were the personas of people, but not the real people at all, only their outer disguise, or should I say they were the constructions their souls had created for themselves in order to function in their respective social environment. These were like garments to cover themselves up with; perhaps unsure about the quality of their nakedness, it was a fragile attempt at projecting a sense of identity which might lend meaning to their lives.

There was the costume of the comedian, or how this person chose to be perceived by his friends. I saw the doting father, the fastidious mother, then the 'bit-of-a-character' persona, all of them fabricated, improvised from a clue of their real individuality which had gone missing somehow for lack of attention to its core reality. I saw how these 'shields' prevented their owners from evolving and shining and manifesting in their everyday world in a pure and simple and honest way, just playing the part they were destined to play with authenticity and joy.

I recognised that these observations were usually conducted from a non-emotional, mental level; deriving insights from there automatically incorporates a deeper understanding.

To me this was not a level to remain tuned in to and so I tuned out and turned off. Instead I picked up on the stillness again and gently began to surrender to it. It had been lingering beneath all appearances as my constant and silent watcher. The true purpose of my meditation was to acknowledge this companion by gently relinquishing thought, sideshows and even insights, no matter how valuable or deep they may appear. I no longer focused on the light either. The light is just a space stripped of thought, a manifestation of being but not pure being itself. Pure being has no attributes at all and when I can feel its presence all I need is to surrender to it.

Eventually I sank into a deep inner peace and stillness without thoughts or attributes; stillness was already there waiting to receive me.

An hour later I rose from my chair, crushed some dry bread I had left out from the night before, and milled it into crumbs with my knuckles. These I cast out onto the veranda. One bird obligingly appeared and carried away a crumb.

Meditation, 9 a.m.

It was still cold. I covered my legs with the soft woollen blanket thoughtfully supplied by the proprietors for which I felt very grateful. As soon as I closed my eyes I sank into a deep relaxed state. I observed in a detached way a pattern of light appearing in front of my closed eyelids, forming and dissolving shapes and vortexes.

From past experience I had learned that observing these can be part of another meditation technique which is often used by lucid dreamers or astral travellers. When followed directly with a special kind of attitude they can develop into hypnagogic imagery and lead us into other worlds while retaining full waking awareness. If practised correctly this technique is often known to trigger wake-induced lucid dreams which then allow excursions into alternate realities, the holy grail of astral travellers.

I did not resist and kept watching without expectation. Soon the beautiful face of a young black woman appeared to my right, smiling at me warmly. She emerged gradually, becoming more defined. She wore a green, sleeveless dress and slowly lifted her slender arm and pointed gracefully, half turning, towards a landscape of light which started to emerge behind her. The scene appeared out of a vortex or a funnel of energy and took on a life of its own. For a moment I watched it unfold, gain depth and clarity. As so often with these kinds of passive visualisations, they work completely independently from the imagination and often surprise with quite unexpected detail which would be a challenge to imagine. The trick for the would-be astral traveller is to allow himself to be passively drawn into the scenery without intent. My heart though sought stillness, and with a warm and heartfelt 'no thank you' I sent the beautiful girl on her way, an almost irresistible invitation yet a distraction nevertheless. The powerful impression of stillness I had experienced towards the end of my last session was still very much present.

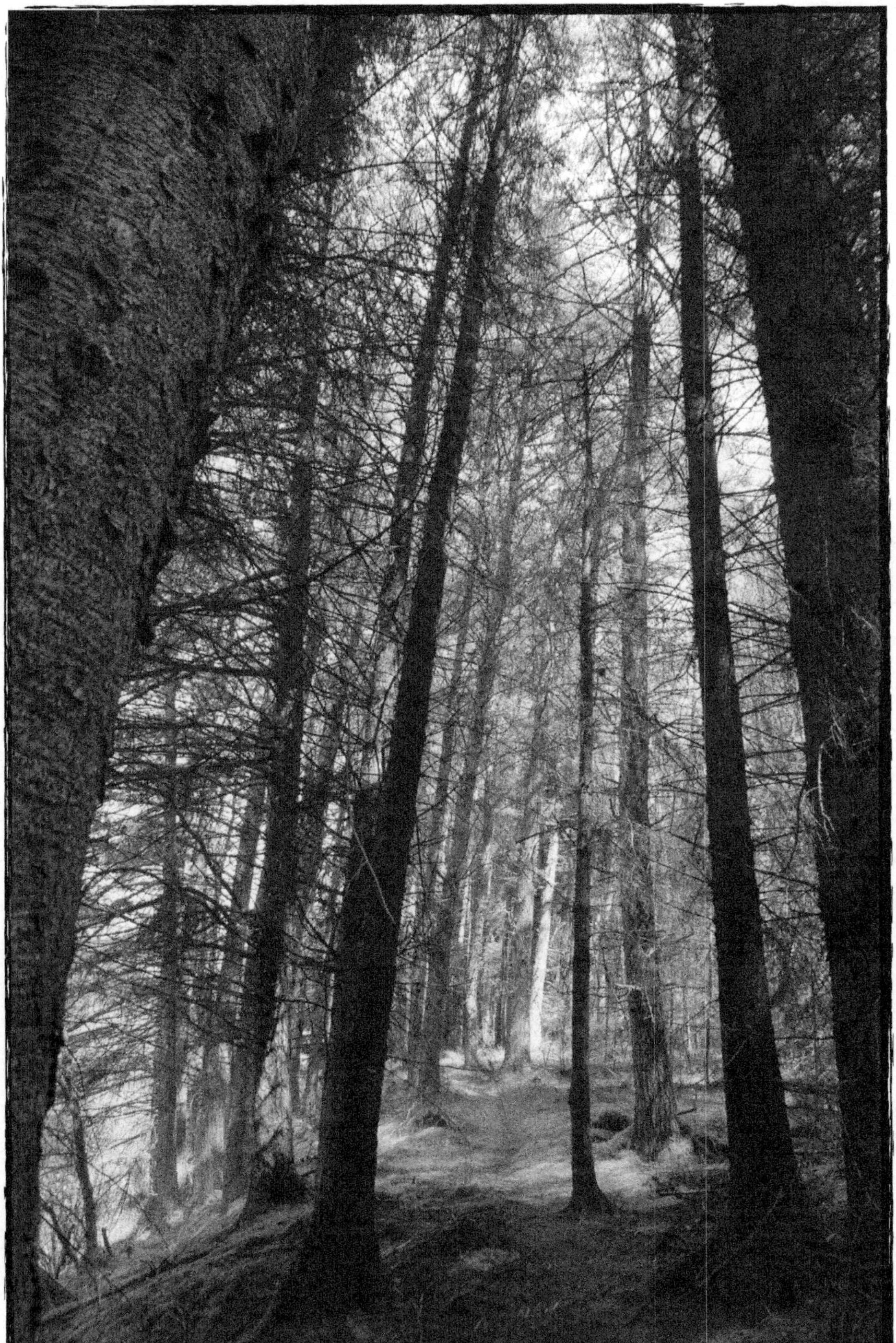

It was not hard to deepen my meditation. I allowed the stillness to settle in the white space above me which I knew was there. It felt like the antechamber to home, the first state of manifestation, the glorious light just as God or consciousness had intended.

I had known of its existence at the outset of my journey; when I experienced it for the first time as a young man it had left a spell on me all my life. Its overwhelming existence was engraved in my history and not at all difficult to focus my attention on. Having found proof of its reality it was not hard to see it as a fact rather than as imagination. All I needed to do now was to place myself into the space again and identify myself with its presence.

I regard meditation as the way, the object, myself and the goal rolled into one. A space for focusing on focus rather than focusing on something that is separate from me. Using a mantra, the light or breathing for focus works best when we become the mantra, the light or the breath. This attitude is important, because it overcomes the illusion that I am separate from the focus of my attention. The 'white space of light' I had become in past meditation is still seen as a living reality, which is not a past event assigned to memory, but a living presence, and all I need to do in my meditation is to realise my identification with it. Why do we cling on to the illusion that we are separate from our thought? That we are an 'I' separated from some 'otherness'? It is pointless focusing on the light when I already know, via foolproof evidence, that I am the light.

But that did not happen this time. Instead another lady appeared to my left in my inner field of vision. She had beautiful brown skin and coffee-brown hair. She was dressed in a colourful

The Ten Minute Moment

Caribbean costume. She smiled seductively at me and pointed with her head towards a golden vortex through which I could clearly see wide open lands basking in golden light, stretching into infinity.

With a grateful smile in my heart I declined. Following her probing invitation I might have travelled heavenly lands while still being the observer, deluded by the vision that I was observer and observed divided. At least in my earlier meditation I had stillness. I was, perhaps only for minutes, engulfed in a void, an experience of intense belonging, of being home, and yet there was not even light, not even a point of light or the promise of it. Light is just a space which exchanges the old physical space with the new non-physical one and despite its glory it means nothing as long as it is perceived as separate from me. Stillness is different even if it is a black void, but as it offers silence, belongingness and unity it is much closer to reality and more powerful than any external experience no matter how glorious.

This however did not materialise this time. If it was that simple we would all be enlightened. Instead I was reminded by excited flapping wings and thrashing very nearby that I was firmly in physical reality, a pair of eyes stuck to a physical body looking at an outside world. Without warning a blue tit had entered the Sheilin through the air vent of my window and was flapping in panic through the room, crashing into windows, perching on top of blinds, taking off noisily and hitting the glass. I jumped up from my meditation position, threw the door wide to offer an escape and then shooed it in the right direction. There was me and there was the bird, two separate beings.

Shortly after, I settled down and entered meditation again. Saving the little feathered fellow had activated my compassion and sympathy and reminded me of my heart. The heart is regarded by some as the most powerful organ in our body and for me it has also become the most powerful instrument in meditation. Using love and compassion it reminds me in a very real feeling way that I am not separated from the world – although my other senses are telling me that I am – but an integral part of it. The heart opens me to joy and it was this I settled on for the next fifty minutes of meditation, just resting in joy. If I want to be connected to the world and not be limited by my physical senses, I try joy.

After my fifty minutes of joy I had tea and toast for breakfast and settled down to write my notes.

Exploration, 11 a.m.

I took my camera and a small backpack with a bottle of water and some fruit I had left over from my journey. I walked down to the road winding along the loch. Clouds had gradually covered the sky, casting shadowless, contrast-poor light. Photographers normally prefer sunlight. I didn't mind though. I was more fascinated by the rotting and moss-covered trees which nature had randomly posted along the edge of the lake. This was a completely new world for me, a new planet even. The artist's mind always welcomes new pastures to graze on and doesn't like repetition, but that's the mind. The heart perceives the world differently. It doesn't record the world in the same way and doesn't compare. The heart is more like a child, willing to see the world as if for the first time, open to experience the old familiar toys in a new and fresh way and it is much more easily engaged. As an artist I have learned to engage my heart first before I start seeing with my eyes. This way I can engage with the world and it communicates with me as if we had never met.

But here my mind had no time for this. This was simply totally new territory. There was just too much to take in and my mind, conditioned for entertainment, started to feast greedily on the new planet which opened up for it. My camera, with a fixed-focus lens, hacked away at the deluge of images floating my way. I hardly had time to rest my eyes, let alone engage my heart. There was just too much to allow me any time to rest and absorb and connect. My mind had entered the Las Vegas of nature.

Inevitably, when I go for the senses and ignore my intuition I pay a price. When I looked at the shots I had taken during my feast of the senses, all the images were out of focus. I had accidentally set the lens for manual. I had been out of synch. I had not been one with my camera. I had wasted time looking without seeing, feasting my eyes without engaging my heart. I had been harvesting without sowing and had not prepared the ground by engaging with my environment. I felt like a fool who had missed a great opportunity. I decided there and then from then on, that every moment had to be my meditation.

I had failed to appreciate the privilege of my experience. I was in the most beautiful part of the world and I had shown no real gratitude for it. I was no more than a tourist who had paid for the trip and now expected to receive the goods he had paid for, the attractions, but who wasn't engaged. I hadn't found myself to be

2 – The Nine-Step Meditation towards Awakening

RADIANCE

Radiance is a manifestation of the light of consciousness, the radiant sun, brighter than all the stars in the universe. I don't have to think about it, just notice it, finding the 'feeling tone' of radiance. When I observe the radiance I surrender to it and allow the radiance to do its thing. It's not me that radiates, but the light of consciousness radiating through me and illuminating everything around me. It is better to let it do this for a few seconds, perhaps minutes, rather than clinging on to it and forcing myself to hold the attention.

Passive attention is allowing consciousness to do this meditation for me. I am no longer a part of it. Consciousness knows how long it wants to show its radiance and I do not have to pursue it. It's like watching a butterfly collecting its nectar. The moment I raise my hands to catch it, it is gone. The radiance of consciousness is like the butterfly. I let it be.

part of it. I was simply a stranger, stumbling from my urban wilderness into this wholesome paradise while totally ignoring the privilege. Worse, I had violated it by my presence, littered it with my arrogance. I had inflicted myself on it, exploiting greedily its resources without even realising my connection. The evidence was there in washed-out blurry images, a truthful reflection of my state of mind and my attitude. I felt ashamed.

I made tea and had a rice cake which I took from a new package discovered in the larder. When I took my first sip I felt gratitude for its warmth, the wholesome feeling of swallowing the comforting brew and feeling the heat of the tea cup warming my hands. I felt forgiven. At least I had managed to connect to the cup of tea. When I took a bite off the rice cake I began to learn appreciation from a basic level. I enjoyed how plain it was. It was simple, light, no added flavourings or spread. The taste of what feeds the body without additives. I felt purified and deeply grateful for its simplicity. With my gratitude came warmth and with warmth finally came a complete appreciation of where I was. I sank onto my chair and looked out into the valley through my open door. Each sip of tea was nourishment for my soul, a thank-you to life, a celebration of where I was.

Meditation, 2 p.m.

So my meditation started while still drinking the tea and taking tiny bites out of my rice cake. Why close my eyes? If meditation is meant to take me to a higher plane I was already here.

My eyes closed by themselves as I lowered the cup to the floor. I could hear birds pecking away at the feeder hung on the entrance post of the Sheilin's veranda. I heard their song and felt it spreading over the hill in front of me, beautiful and pure and so in tune with the gentle rushing of the wind moving the levees of the trees and bushes to underscore the melodies.

But I was tired. A drowsiness crept in and with it thoughts began to invade, the kind of thoughts which would morph into dream fragments and then into dreams. I tried to stay awake. Morning meditation is so much sharper and focused. I sought stillness, but instead thoughts, uninteresting and random, were clamouring for attention, a sure sign of tiredness. My heart was not engaged either. It had already sought sanctuary in a different place. I dragged myself away from the shadowy fragments clouding my mind, hoping to find some clarity somewhere I could latch on to in order to wake me up, but my body had other ideas. As it slumped forward it jolted me into momentary wakefulness, but not for very long. The second time my chin hit my chest I dragged myself to my feet and fell onto my bed into dreamless sleep

Meditation, 3 p.m.

Heavy rain clouds had drifted into the valley from the west. I had got up refreshed from my nap and was now sitting at my desk to record the day's events in my diary. A gentle rain was drumming against the windows. And as I looked up through the window a deer, graceful and unperturbed by the rain, grazed its way slowly up the hill, a few yards away from my hut.

The Ten Minute Moment

I brewed a cup of green tea then opened the door and sat down in my meditation place facing the valley. This had now become a permanent fixture. There could be no better place with a more magnificent view in the whole world. I felt really blessed and privileged beyond words. The view revealed a horseshoe shape of silver birch foliage and the grass, which had the rich vitality of late-spring green. Through this aperture I had a glimpse of the lake and beyond, along its shore, more patches and lines of tree abundance climbing up the steep slopes of the mountain, conifers stopping just short of the top, which was covered in varying shades of green mosses and grass. The white clouds travelling high above had begun to make room for a blue sky and now varying shadows passed over this landscape, igniting the green with more saturated colour and flinging yellow sparks of light into the air where it was struck by the sun.

A band of cumulus giants marched across the tops, relentlessly carrying the burden of heavy rain to come. As children we would have projected our fantasy worlds into their morphing and ever-changing shapes. Looking at them now I felt that time had not moved on since childhood, as my dreamy mind leisurely painted shapes into the clouds.

Soon I began losing count of my stock of creations, as a half-elephant half-camel marched along the hilltop while morphing into two talking heads. There is no need to meditate with your eyes shut when you can witness creation at work first hand and ponder the powers which give it life.

Now the wind had dropped but not the busy chatter of the birds, the wings of one flapping past so fast that I missed it. Another little fellow had settled in front of me just outside the door, picking up crumbs, taking off and coming back for more.

Just like the mind can change, the weather and the atmosphere are like the mind of our earth and can change just as quickly. Here it altered when a lumbering grey cloud decided to cut off all the sunlight. It orchestrated a soundtrack by raining tiny droplets onto millions of little leaves which rustled under the sudden charge, clinging tightly to their branches, swaying in unison, whispering loudly to each other.

Then it was silent again but not for long. The wind started talking through the trees and it's difficult to say why the wind and trees should in any way be separate from one another.

Looking through my eyes, then through the door into an outside world, it would almost be foolish to consider that beauty has to be found inside. As yet I had still to determine where the inside stopped and the outside began. There appears to no longer be an 'anywhere', the moment when the mind contemplates unity. Here the different aspects of nature merged and united, while the clouds with their swift movements kept documenting the transience of it all. What was the origin of this unfolding drama and what is behind it? How different are the thoughts which created the majestic mountain from the humble thoughts inside my head which observe and comment on all this?

When I close my eyes for meditation I can rest assured that the forest on its mountain and the lake beneath it are still there. Seamlessly they migrate from the outside and slip behind my closed eyelids as an imprint in my mind. They assume new powers and begin to transform and take on their new identity. No longer burdened by their history, in my mind the green grass now sprouts red-golden tips and the whole country beyond lights up, bringing an inner light to bear on the scene. What previously had been clouds of water vapour now effortlessly morph and unite with the mountain, creating new features of another world. Even the sounds and the singing of the birds seeps into my inner world, adding tiny features with their sound, each note creating shapes.

Quietly the soundscape is enhanced by the noise coming from my stomach. Opening my eyes and watching the little chaffinch picking up the crumbs on my patio, I am reminded that I am a physical being too and in need of some food myself.

When shown to the larder on my arrival I just grabbed vegetables at random. Without thinking or planning I somehow figured that this would be all I could consume in one week. There was an inhibiting factor at work too: the fact that I was in a retreat run by devoted community of Buddhists and that the food I took was free. It is an interesting paradox that things which are free have the potential power of stopping greed. Tonight, however, was my first home-cooked meal.

Day three, Sunday 2 June
Illusion and Reality

I got up relatively late, at 6 a.m. Strange how I seem to start every day with a clean sheet as if the mind employs dreams in order to wipe away the remnants of the previous day. Throwing open the door I was greeted by a fresh morning with a few clouds spread out like a quilt over the land, gently pulled to one side by a silent breath of wind.

The previous day I had observed a red squirrel checking me out, a new intruder on its territory. Was I friendly? When I grabbed my camera to take a quick shot of him, he disappeared so quickly that I only caught his fleeing tail. The photo I captured gave him his name, Tails. Where I come from red squirrels are a rare species. Today I had the camera ready with the long zoom lens. To entice more company I had also squeezed a piece of rice cake into the bird feeder, but it didn't attract a lot of interest. I then discovered a jar of sunflower and pumpkin seeds in the larder. I grabbed a handful and laid it out on the veranda. This was more popular.

Tails came first. He was more convinced by my good intentions now and that I didn't pose a threat. My door was wide open and I slowly eased the camera onto my lap, hoping not to scare the little red fellow away with this large gun-like shooter. No need to worry, he threw me a few glances then worked his way methodically through the kernels from right to left, occasionally throwing me an eye, checking whether I could be trusted. When he first heard the camera shutter he froze into takeoff position, but then carried on. Considerately he offered different poses, a photographer's dream: sitting up, his hands humanlike holding a kernel, mouth to the ground; sideways, frontal, back view, like a fashion model posing for

Vogue. I was pleased with the shots and the squirrel took it in its stride. Quite casual now, I grinned, Tails now more relaxed as I clicked away.

Watching Tails at his breakfast I started estimating the size of his stomach and calculated whether the portions would see him through the day. I fetched some more supplies, after all it was Sunday. Birds now arrived from everywhere, but the red squirrel was only in it for himself. Not that he was mean or selfish. He was just bigger and didn't even have to prove it.

Meditation, 7 a.m.

My meditation started much later than yesterday. I decided to use a technique I hadn't tried for a while, self-enquiry.

'What am I?' By asking the question I focused on that which asked the question. It is important to get to the feeling that is behind the question. This question can be linked to other questions which may more readily produce results such as, 'What am I?'

'What is this me and what is it made of?'

'Who is doing the meditation?'

'What is it that makes me be me?'

I left the questions unanswered, suspended in the air, there to be taken up by something that knew the answer. Then in my mind's eye I saw a bright golden semi-disc, like a rising sun over the horizon, a bright orange rim.

'Who is watching the sun?' I queried. The sun faded and left behind stillness, a deep inner peace without any questions. My inner vision became brighter, illuminated and filled all space around me.

'Who is observing the luminous space?'

The space dissolved and then I was consumed by wide open emptiness with nothing to observe, a void, just a state of being and total stillness . . .

When I opened my eyes again an hour had passed.

I started hour two with Qi Gong. I was stiff, straight out of bed without any exercise whatsoever. After fifteen minutes body and soul felt more balanced. I was surprised that after the self-enquiry meditation, which had resulted in such prolonged immersion in stillness, I was able to hold my standing meditation on one leg for so long without the slightest wobble. Normally I tend to sway to and fro a little, but this time I was keenly aware that not only was my mind completely quiet but as a direct result my body was equally so too.

The second meditation turned out to be quite different. I decided to simply observe, detached and uninvolved, whatever showed up in front of my vision. In the past this technique has occasionally led to spontaneous out-of-body experiences. Though rare, they would lead me into alternate realities. There I would deepen my waking awareness and be able to fully immerse myself into another world or even universe. This state also tends to make it much easier to enter very deep states of meditation, without losing awareness. Tibetan monks use it and author Stephen LaBerge recommends it to induce lucid dreaming from waking. The idea is to invite hypnagogic images while keeping yourself uninvolved. The images slowly morph from flashes of light on the retina to patterns projected on the inner shields of the eyelids. There they attract new shapes and then invite content from the subconsciousness to rise to the surface. This could be anything, from faces to complete scenes. Their key characteristic is that they are unintended, nor are they imagined, but rise to the surface on their own account. Using this method, with the right attitude which was close to a dream yet with the mind still awake I could enter the scenes and immerse myself and then take control. This would provide the starting base for multidimensional journeys like portals into parallel realities.

It was important not to be out for anything or expecting results. This is not how consciousness works. I needed to behave like watching the squirrel, pretending not to be interested and allowing the scenes to do their own thing. By pretending not to be directly engaged with the squirrel I allowed it to remain undisturbed and feed naturally. Nature is nature and consciousness is nature too. Nature is constant throughout. Here I employed my inner camera stealthily, as a passive tool for recording. It was important to remain unengaged and yet passively alert. Consciousness is just as fickle as the birds on my veranda and, just as the birds, it appreciates remaining undisturbed while feeding. Consciousness feeds like the birds, is continuously on the lookout for food, to expand, to feast on new information and opportunities. It is like the grazing deer in front of my Sheilin, shy and fickle. My food for consciousness was space and a blank canvas it could use to expand into.

The Ten Minute Moment

With my self-consciousness deactivated and intentions gone I soon observed plenty of abstract shapes emerging, fractal patterns, but they were little more than morphing wallpaper, of interest perhaps to a textile designer, but fascinating to observe that they had their own unknown design source.

Keeping more focused on not getting too involved, becoming a non-participating observer, I allowed it more space. Then, slowly, my attention was drawn to my heart as if the heart was telling me that it too was consciousness and was gently taking the initiative without me doing anything. The new focus of consciousness was highly meaningful and wholesome and very powerful in its giving as I observed it filling the space I left. At the same time I was rewarded with new hypnagogic visions inciting me to let go. Instead of the pattern, I was now observing a snowy landscape and was drawn straight into it. As I drew closer I found it brightly lit, much brighter than the daylight at noon. At the same time I became aware of an important yet subtle transition in consciousness, which had a dreamlike signature, but being fully aware it was also beyond dream and became hyper-real. Momentarily I entered this scene, still holding on to a part of physical awareness, and then gently began to follow the brightly lit path. I knew full well that if I didn't waver and was not distracted in any way I could simply use this gateway and allow consciousness to lure me into its native playing field, a parallel universe in full waking awareness, a reality vivid and vital, more so than physical wakefulness.

For a moment my inner adventurer rose to the bait. I was caught and taken into unknown lands, new territories never visited before, and I could already see that these were of a much higher luminous world. These were lands ready for me to enter without much to do in terms of personal transition. It was a land beyond emotion, beyond identification or attachment and I was ready to enter. I could see already as I set foot onto the white path, that it would lead me to a new unknown, into incomprehensible realms. Lands with an atmosphere never before encountered yet like a forgotten memory. A realm missed for aeons but only now finding out that it was missed.

Laid out in front of me was heaven, containing long-forgotten times, remembered pleasures and visual delights, changing and exhilarating with every step. I was blessed with an opportunity I had silently hoped for before I planned my retreat, that I would find my way into the highest levels of awareness which I could then explore to the full and on my return then write about. But it wasn't what my heart had in store. My heart spoke from a different place.

'Who is seeing the path? Who wants to follow into the world of heaven?'

'Who?'

I was stopped in my tracks. I considered that my early self-inquiry had not gone deep enough and now consciousness simply picked up where it had left off. All that was on offer by following the call of the heart was silence and no promise, but also total surrender to a stillness beyond words.

I could not ignore it and I chose stillness, a state without intent or desire, just being. I felt this was the only way I could get closer to what is, to what reality is in its essence rather than the images it presents, the images of the world, imagined heavens, the presentation of its creation, and I felt blessed when making this choice.

Better than considering an ideal was to become real and humbly accepting what I am with all its limitations. There were no attributes that could make me into anything special, make me stand out, and in that I perceived the greatest blessing, to be as humble as the squirrel on my porch, as the bird feeding on the crumbs given to them. The pleasure was intense and so was the gratitude I felt.

My eyes opened to the world around me. I stood up and attended to my body. I had two slices of toast which I divided into four pieces. On three of them I spread honey, marmalade on the remaining one. I made a cup of tea and then another.

Meditation, 10 a.m.

After clearing breakfast away and finishing my household chores I settled down for my third meditation session of the day. For a few minutes I pondered how beautiful it was to have such freedom. I looked through the open door onto the magnificent abundance nature was offering to me and I felt deep gratitude for this privilege. In response my body leaned forward involuntarily, bowing to the greater authority of the world before my eyes, manifested in the grass, the trees, the mountains and the song of the birds.

I could never have been any good at following an order or a community of monks, I thought. I would have been too self-

3 – The Nine-Step Meditation towards Awakening

UNITY

Unity is the third meditation. I have noticed love and it has noticed me. Consciousness sends love to radiate out. When the two are truly merged they find unity. I notice, observe and feel the unity and I can feel it closely, because I am surrendered to the unity which is taking place inside me. I don't think about unity. I just balance and suspend the word in front of me, featherlike, without effort. I do not need to think about it. All I need to do is notice its reality and simply surrender to unity. That's all I need to do. Even if it is only for a few seconds. Length of time is not an issue because where unity is there is no time and when it leaves it leaves. I am unity.

conscious and, yes, too self-important. The good thing about being on a solitary retreat was that I didn't have to follow anything at all, only my impulses, a bit of common sense and the gentle persuasions of the heart to pursue beauty which made no demands. All choices were mine. I thought how easy it would be to apply these directives to everyday life, how little could go wrong if my first port of call in any situation would simply be to love. How could I ever be touched or reproached as I would always be following the silent directives of love, of my heart, without the need to judge and only to give with open intent.

I saw that love followed its own rules. The rules of society are still there, but if I were to follow the inner wisdom of love they would no longer apply to me. The wisdom of the heart takes precedence. It is a law unto itself and would not be breaking any rules. Rules are like distant manifestations with little relevance to me as I would simply do what was right without having to run it past the mind for judgement. And what freedom life would have to offer if I was no longer restricted by its rules. People exposed to, holding and giving such love, I pondered, would instinctively accept that deep down there is only the one law that counts and it governs all life, from the lowest atom to its highest galaxy in this universe.

'Yes', I thought when I became aware of my thoughts, 'this is how thoughts smooth their way into my meditation and just because they are beautiful and elevated they con me into thinking that I was meditating, when in fact I was just distracted. Thoughts are insidious, taking on disguises and undermining the heart by pretending to be the heart. I have seen it too many times and yet still fall victim to them.'

This is the way of thoughts, how they evolve and progress, how they paint an ideal world and yet miss reality by miles. How they deceive in letting me believe that I am meditating. How they make me feel good while ruling the roost. This was not meditation at all and I had to remind myself that the only thing real at present was to acknowledge the birds in front of me, hacking at the seeds I had spread out for them, popping from spot to spot, picking and nodding and dancing and flapping and flying off. Only this was real; and observing this, how is that not meditation?

To accept that I had become a bird watcher without obsessing with detail, that was meditation. The sound of their little plasticky feet on the dry wood and the rustling leaves in the background were far more real and hence much more enticing than to ponder the deeper meanings of love and life or even to consider what species these little fellows might belong to.

I decided it was time to venture out into the world rather than waste my time considering purposes or meanings or who I was. I had arrived in a world which had been carved out of paradise and I was sitting here wasting my time with pointless pondering. So I packed a banana and a bottle of water into my little rucksack together with a notepad. I decided not to take my whole camera kit and just mounted the short but heavy zoom lens to the body. I wrapped the strap securely around my wrist and held it by the grip so it was ready to shoot.

I had hardly walked fifty yards down the hill through the high grass when I saw a tiny fawn collapsed on the overgrown track right in front of me. As I got a little closer it scrambled to its feet pathetically but instantly collapsed a couple of feet later into the high grass where it lay motionless.

I looked around for its mother, but she was nowhere to be seen. While I was considering what to do with a motionless fawn I took a picture, as I only had to press the trigger, but that was just stalling for time. I still had no idea what I should do in such situation. I had heard stories that the mothers of wild animals sometimes rejected their young when they had been in contact with humans. I took another good look around to see if the mother was anywhere near, but she wasn't. I considered the fact that the fawn may have been injured, hence the collapse when it tried to get up. From where I stood I checked it over to see if there were any superficial injuries or traces of blood in the grass. Then I crouched right down to have a closer look, but I could not find anything. I wanted to talk to it, ask questions, but could only focus on my heart, helpless and inept, though it raised a powerful feeling of compassion. I thought if I touched it gently and briefly it would simply take off if it was OK. So I did, but it didn't respond. I then gently stroked it, first its soft back, then its tiny head with those large and sad-looking dark eyes.

I considered the fact that it might have suffered a broken leg. I nudged it gently then raised it up to its feet to see if it would hobble off, but it just stood frozen. At least it didn't collapse. I then was convinced that the time had come to intervene and take action. I lifted the little fellow off the ground and into my arms. His legs were very spindly, disproportionately long and fell awkwardly crisscrossed over my arms. I gently tried to fold them into a more natural position until I was cradling the little deer like newborn baby.

It was only when I considered what help was needed that the thought struck me that I had adopted this orphan and that it would automatically become my responsibility and, yes, my burden, to look after it, nurse it with a bottle until a sanctuary had been found. I felt extremely sorry for it, having lost its parent so young, and I wondered how I could possibly compensate for such a loss. I also couldn't look past the uncomfortable thought that I would have to sacrifice my freedom and self-interest in such a scenario. But cradling this tiny warm body in my arms I felt a surge of instinctive compassion and overwhelming love, wishing with all my heart that whatever I was able to do would be enough to put things right again.

At that moment the fawn struggled, kicked violently and let out a piercing scream as it tried to struggle free. Instinctively and without hesitation I lowered it gently to the ground. It leaped up vigorously, bounced through the high grass up the hill and disappeared into the bushes.

The Ten Minute Moment

'What was that all about?' I thought. Fawn-less and answerless I proceeded down the hill and turned west along the lake when I reached the road.

I was relieved that things had turned out so well. That the sun had come out properly now, that it was shining on me and by doing so was letting me know that everything would be OK and that the fawn, miraculously, would be OK too, and that the world was good and OK and a kind place to live. This was one of life's little adventures that was teaching me that everything would be all right.

A short distance later I saw a sign, two miles to the hotel. The girl I had given a lift on my arrival had told me that sometimes residents from the retreat centre would make the walk in order to have tea or to 'escape' as she put it with a smirk. At that time I was more preoccupied with marvelling at the beautiful scenery, but now I found she had actually planted a thought into my head, a seed of appealing desire.

Somehow the thought of having a proper meal after three days began to work its magic. I soon discovered that with the idea in my head it seemed to lighten my step and made the day appear a lot sunnier than it already was. On my way, however, the scenery began to play with me more and more and I made use of my camera to capture it and freeze it in time so I would never lose it again. I became a 'scene picker' like a farmer harvesting apples. My camera became my basket. With eager eyes I hunted for the best crop, picked out the best compositions, the highest-yielding patches. I darted from spot to spot to find the best angle for exploitation and greedily absorbed where the lights and shadows were at their most effective.

Soon I became dissatisfied with the bright noon sunlight and started to complain about its lack of subtlety. I accused it of being bland and spoiling the scenery and in the end decided to let it go. I only harvested a few more shots, but they were no more than memory cards, a reminder that I had been here and, if I wanted, at least I could go back in my mind and ponder what could have been.

An hour and a half had gone by when I arrived at the hotel having pocketed my fill of picture-postcard content safely inside my camera.

At least I had picked a great part of the season and time of the year when the landscape's bright June greens had turned everything I had come across into an exuberant idyll. Slowly I was won back by the gentle warmth of the sun, the brightly lit scenery with its saturated colours. From deep inside me it evoked hidden memories from unworldly places, memories akin to out-of-body experiences I had had in the past. I felt like I was on some astral plane without having had to leave my body. I was in the borderlands of heaven and could even sense its bliss, such beauty. Inner and outer began to merge and it was difficult to hold these two realities apart. Without really quite absorbing it I had been walking through paradise for an hour, though now my feet gently started to remind me that I had a very physical body.

The hotel consisted of a postcard cottage, walls in a pink wash and a beautifully kept lawn, flowing almost down to the edge of the lake. By the time I made it to the hotel driveway leading over the cattle grid I had already cooked a Sunday dinner in my head. As I reached its terrace I began to make my selection from an imaginary sweet trolley and by the time I was ready to deposit my order at the reception desk I had already chosen the wine. Instead of further taxing my imagination, for simplicity's sake it was ordinary house red.

I entered the lobby via the conservatory, which was actually the restaurant. I had noticed that the guests and the place had an air of exclusivity and there I was, slightly exhausted, the camera slung around my shoulder, a scruffy old backpack and trousers and probably an obvious sweat stain on my back, anything other than an appealing dinner guest. I was also deliberately ignored and then was skilfully intercepted by the waiter before I even had a chance to open my mouth.

The Ten Minute Moment

'I am sorry, sir, all our Sunday dinners are pre-booked, but you are welcome to a light soup or sandwiches in the bar or the lounge.'

By that time I had entered the bar, which was like a pitch-black hole as my eyes tried to adjust from the bright sunlight to the darkness; all I could see was the edge of the bar and a glint of the highlights of the spirit bottles behind, but nothing else apart from the waiter's gleaming white jacket and his teeth.

Shunning the darkness I opted for the lounge. Judging by his accent the waiter must have been from Eastern Europe. He could have been a friend of the Lithuanian girl I had given a lift to on my arrival. He was very polite and very clean in contrast to me, a weary wanderer, a one-day hermit, roughed up by the weather after an hour and a half of walking in the sun. There were just three extra tables with casual chairs, tastefully selected as if they had always been part of the old lounge.

I ordered a bottle of sparkling water and a smoked chicken sandwich on freshly home-baked bread. When it arrived it also had smoked salmon and crème fraiche added to it and was artistically garnished with lettuce and beautifully presented. I felt amply compensated for my lack of Sunday dinner and it was much more fitting for a new hermit like myself.

By the time I came to make my way back it had become quite hot and I stuffed my jumper into my rucksack, strapped my camera securely around my right wrist, ready for shooting and set off on my path home. Facing the opposite way I was assured that I would enter a completely new world.

The Ten Minute Moment

There is a benefit in the walking meditation of the photographer. The key is to avoid thought and instead focus on the heart as the aperture for finding images and motives. The mind will only see what it has seen before and the photographs are likely to be repetitive, predictable and boring. Thoughts take their raw material from what is known and rarely ever discover anything new. Thoughts live in the past but the heart takes its sustenance from the present. It scours beauty and feasts on rhythms, symmetry and the undiscovered. To see with the heart means to put everything I know about photography to one side and allow myself to be connected to the present and be open to surprises.

I was drawn towards the water's edge with its unpredictable features. The fallen trees covered in moss, ready to be recycled by nature, their roots reaching like begging arms into the sky. After a while the camera became forgotten. It became a heavy appendage handcuffed to my arm and served no purpose. Instead I was taken in by the summer air, the wind which blew gentle kisses in my face. The warmth of the sun with its white silvery light played on my skin and when I stopped and closed my eyes I could still see the afterimage of its powerful light. Inside and outside were connected, light everywhere. I was close to home, my real home, which was in my heart.

My heart had taken a different route. The light summer breath and the sun could not be photographed, only enjoyed. When I opened my eyes tentatively, after having rested on a mossy rock, I had gently been escorted into paradise, an astral realm, where the vibrant green of the June trees had just been released and refreshed moment by moment. The light branches waving 'thank you' to the wind, and the water with its harmonic silent ripples, confirmed their own gratitude. It was left to the birds to provide the sound score and they did so perfectly, not a note out of place.

After dreamily stumbling over rocks and climbing over fallen trees, avoiding little streams emptying their crystal content into the lake, I climbed up the embankment to find an easier route home on the smooth surface of the road, but instead of finding an easy path I stepped into a pothole hidden by the shadow of a tree and camouflaged by leaves. My right foot twisted at a sharp angle and the weight of my body followed suit. There was no stopping now. I foresaw my head hitting the road and it was only my right hand strapped to the camera which could prevent the impact. A moment

The Ten Minute Moment

later the camera, all two thousand pounds' worth of it, slammed into the tarmac, but I was saved as I rolled over my right shoulder to the side of the road with barely a scratch. The only thing affected was my ankle.

I propped myself up against a tree. With my eyes shut I savoured the pain in my foot. It sent electric spasms through my body and I waited until they calmed. The most unpleasant sound was the metallic thud from the camera as it hit the road. Expecting the worst, I lifted it to eye level, with its strap still twisted tightly around my wrist, and inspected the damage. The lens had escaped unharmed, but a massive scar had ruptured its black skin and revealed the silver of its titanium body.

It looked alarming, but there was hope. In the past I had dropped it, left it in the snow and even had used it in heavy rain. It was designed for war zones and it had survived this time as well. Everything was functioning and the chink in its armour, added to the paint on the grip when shooting during a painting session, simply added to its pedigree. I was relieved and grateful.

What or who was to blame for my misfortune? Was it my indulgence of a craving for a Sunday dinner, consuming the best sandwich in the world as the poor monk I set out to be? Or was it simply because I had deserted my heart which had navigated me so skilfully along the water's edge and instead following my mind seeking the easy route along the plain tarmac? But feeling my pain I already felt forgiven.

Gently, I tested my foot. It hurt but was not broken. I took a few steps and then stopped, assessing the level of pain. I felt the earth underneath it, the solid ground. I allowed the pain to seep into the ground, like a burden emptying its load. I slowly did so with every new step and gradually increased my pace. Fifty more steps and the pain had eased. A couple of hundred yards later it had gone. Instead I felt a sting in my left hand and when I looked it still showed a red imprint of the rough tarmac, but as I watched I saw it melt away. It was all in my mind.

Was this a dream, then, an unmanifested probability? The marks on my camera said no.

Back home in my Sheilin temple I opened the door with the view on the mountain for my afternoon meditation. Yes, the world was a dream as it rested in the afternoon sun. There once was a little fawn lost on a hill without its mother, aeons ago, another era. The mountain had seen it all, many times over, countless stories and fates, and not a dent was left in it. I admired its stillness, its solitude, its unwavering character, come rain, come snow, millennia after millennia. I admired its stillness until I too became still. Stillness decides what hurts and what doesn't and nothing was hurting as my eyes closed in peace. My heart responded, sending me its gratitude and its joy. I had little else to offer in response other than to share. I then sank into an infinite calm, so deep that I disappeared from the world.

4 – The Nine-Step Meditation towards Awakening

WELL-BEING

Well-being results out of such unity. How can it be anything else? I do not even have to think about it, just become aware and surrender to its reality. Health and well-being have resulted from this great outpouring of consciousness. Well-being is the fountain of creation and manifestation. I do not think of well-being in terms of its opposition to sickness. Sickness does not even enter my mind. Well-being is simply an attribute of the powerful light of consciousness I can feel. I can feel it inside me travelling through every atom of my body. It is very subtle and knows exactly where to go. It doesn't need me or my guidance. I simply let well-being be until it decides. I simply observe it with gratitude.

I pick up the word like this two or three times and then simply let it go naturally.

Day four, Monday 3 June
The Alternative Life

I got up at 4:30 a.m. I opened the blinds, the curtain and then the door to the outside, letting in the scenery, but the morning greeting me was grey and cold. In the distance a heavy cloud gripped the mountain like the hand of a titan or an ancient god. The leftover rice I had laid out on a lid and placed on the veranda had almost gone and the little dish had been moved to one side by its feeders.

The morning looked stark and had a powerful presence of everyday reality, even in this exalted landscape. Then I noticed in surprise that my right foot was hurting. When I examined it the ankle was badly swollen. Reality announced its return. I wondered whether my heart had been fooling me the day before and in my euphoria my body chemistry had blessed me with endorphin taking away the pain; a cold and rational analysis, as cold as the morning. The beautiful scenery, the initial euphoria and the novelty of this retreat had left no room for pain, for reality. The romance with nature, its teeming beauty, the elevating meditation and the effect of it, all gone, replaced by the grey light of reality. I had been fooled. I had been the victim of illusion. The reality was that I was simply out in the wild, where nature was in a more sombre mode. With the miracle of spontaneous healing gone, where the body had been conned into a false sense of security, I began to realise that my heart had skilfully orchestrated a world of deception around me and of wishful thinking.

I sat down on my chair, manoeuvring my foot into a more comfortable position. I began to ponder the fate of the fawn, which I seemed to have so miraculously healed and helped on its feet to find its way home. What might have happened to it? In search of its mother, deprived of her milk and weakened, it could have fallen victim to the foxes patrolling the open.

In the worst-case scenario I considered the idea that, yes, foxes too had a right to live, as a comforting thought, but it did not work. My heart was not convinced and instead I was close to tears. What is reality? Is it good or is it bad? The pain in my foot with its swelling was letting me know that I might have to endure it for the rest of my stay in this mountainous paradise, reminding me every moment that life was hurtful, pitted with suffering and that reality was indifferent to good intentions or idealistic thoughts.

The rain began to comment on my feelings, first gently, then more violently releasing its plunder. I stared thoughtless through its haze, watched the branches shudder under the rainy might and the birds fall silent.

The Ten Minute Moment

Half an hour later it had stopped reluctantly. I got to my feet and limped clumsily to the veranda. To my right, stepping forlornly through the grass, I saw the mother deer. Momentarily my heart bounced into action as I peered out for the fawn, but I could not see it. The mother was on her own. I took my camera with the telephoto lens to scan the grass, inch by inch, from left to right and from right to left again and then again. There was no fawn.

I lowered my camera, still looking, still hoping. I watched the mother slowly walk her route, chewing the wet grass, lifting her head watching me, then meandering off into the growth without her offspring.

I felt betrayed. I tried to find reconciliation in a cup of green tea. I was not hungry. As I sat down I surrendered to its warming comfort. My mind was still, but it was a sad stillness. My sadness had no peace. It was robbed by an absent fawn, a mother who had lost her child, and my foot which throbbed quietly in pain, a shallow pain, a reminder of what was real, a silent commentary on life's ambivalence. There was no rising sun, only a blanket of colourless grey, evenly cheating the world of all life. The vibrant June green of the foliage was stripped away and had turned into monotonous ash.

Yes, reality, I mused. Throughout my life I had shown a soft spot for reality. I had learned that only reality can open the door to truth. I had been its respectful admirer, its faithful servant. It had taught me and assured me that it would never let me down and always faithfully strip me of all illusion. I could rely on it. Reality can never end and if it did it would always be there in the end, when all illusion and dreams had run their course. The lost fawn, the deprived mother, my painful foot, the rain, the mountain, the cup of tea, its shallow comfort, my heavy heart, the memories; reality at work.

Over the years I had forged a bond with it and long surrendered, frequently rebelling, sometimes cursing but in the end I handed myself over and asked for nothing in return. Occasionally I found a smile inside when it showed me the transience of all things. All things, whether good or bad, will come to an end, just as the rain had finally stopped.

When I sought the retreat I had not sought a retreat from reality. I had come here to fling myself open to whatever would come my way without expectation. There was nothing good and nothing bad, it was just the way it was; who am I to judge the processes which had set it all in motion?

The Ten Minute Moment

There was stillness beyond its motion and its changing exterior. The first day I entered this little shrine I found an altar with the wooden statue of the Buddha. I moved him to my desk together with the two candles placed on either side where I wrote my journal. He also watched me eating my meals and when I went to bed and rose up in the morning. He had become my guardian of reality rather than my focus of attention for worship. When meditating I faced the opposite way, the world outside away from the altar. There had been nothing to retreat from but everything to turn to.

I meditated for two and a half hours observing the greyness of the morning and slowly finding my peace with it. My eyes looked inwards where grey thoughts were grazing on an injured heart.

They raised the big questions. What is behind all suffering? But there were no answers. Eventually I left it to my heart to ponder the big question and it simply succumbed to compassion and then to peace.

Dreaming, 7:20 a.m.

I went back to bed without undressing, simply lying flat on my back covered with a light blanket. I enjoyed the weight of my body gently falling away as I kept my attention focused on what 'is'. Then I was carried away into a dream, soft and gentle. I saw flower beds and a lawn surrounded by bushes and I sat on a garden chair at a small cast-iron table flanked by two ladies, who were chatting with each other. With curiosity I gradually began to learn that I was no longer in a dream. As has happened so often in the past, after early morning meditation, going back to bed could result in a lucid dream. I had long learned to regard such dreams as cues to establish full waking consciousness without waking physically and as I observed the minute detail of the forged metal table, my mind attained total waking clarity.

All my adult life I had regarded lucid dreams as gateways into a greater reality, parallel worlds, and had kept journal entries for over forty years of hundreds of such events. I later chronicled them in my book 'Multidimensional Man'. These experiences enabled me to enter and explore higher dimensions of reality in full waking consciousness. Once there, I was able to visit and communicate with relatives who had passed away years before. Nature has provided us with a natural way of exploring the wider territories of our consciousness, which doesn't require magic, religion, prayer, sorcery or occult rituals. Nature has given us our dreams. Every night she opens the door for us with an invitation, which we mostly prefer to ignore, having our sense of reality firmly fastened on our physical body and senses, ignoring one of nature's greatest gifts.

Not only do we have the potential to awaken in our dreams and take an active part in them, we can change them and pacify our greatest fears. We can use our dreams to transform our lives and heal our ills, but we choose not to. And yet lucid dreams are only the beginning of the incredible power and potential consciousness has to offer. We can transcend our dreams altogether and enter much higher states of consciousness, where our waking experience surpasses anything we can experience in our physical bodies.

The Ten Minute Moment

Over the years I had learned to regard these alternative realities with respect and cherish the wealth and abundance they had to offer. Meeting these two ladies now in full waking awareness was no different than meeting old friends in a café back in the everyday world. And that's what they were, old friends I had never met before in my life. At least the older lady I recognised instantly on a deep level.

Instead of assuming full control of the opportunity and following my own whims of exploration, I had learned a long time ago that consciousness puts me into certain places for a reason, often to show or even teach me something. So I remained quietly in my chair, listening intently to the older lady holding the floor. I figured she was in her seventies. Her face was lined. Her hair was dyed blond, but it did not look unnatural. She had just maintained what had always been hers and it didn't look out of place. She was intelligent, I could see that instantly. She made witty observations, occasionally with a sprinkle of sarcasm, but never unkind. I found her matter-of-fact attitude deeply appealing as she commented on life's intrigues and surprises, and remarked that not all of life's treasures could be realised in one go. She looked at me and I understood that her last comment was directed at my presence. I caught softness and a kind of mellowness which came close to resignation when her eyes caught mine. The noon sun caught a tear appearing just at the corners. She looked away.

I was moved by her voice and wanted to say something but had no words. The more I sat in her presence the more I realised that I knew her, not just casually but on a deep level. I had memories of us which I could not formulate. I looked at her face as she glanced down. Her companion gently touched her hand and she took it. I saw her face now from a new angle and I began to recognise it. She had been young and very attractive once and I could see it through all the lines which covered her face evenly. She was well presented and I could see that she had strived to maintain her looks throughout her life into old age with pride and dignity. Not a line and not a hair were out of place. Her posture was supported by an inner nobility as a result of meeting life's challenges and adversities successfully, although her small round face was not the most obvious sign of this.

My confusion grew with every moment as I realised with more certainty that I had known her and yet there was no trace of memory I could clearly relate to. When she looked at me I asked:

'How do I know you?'

'You would have known me had you not moved to England and met your young wife.'

I was shocked; perhaps I did know her after all and I enquired about her name.

'My name is Jung, but that won't mean anything to you as we have never met, at least not in this lifetime. And no, I am not a distant relative of Carl Gustav,' she said with a cheeky smile.

I was awestruck by the philosophical implications of what would have been had I made different choices in my life, had I not decided to go to England. Slowly an alternative life began to roll up in front of me where I had met another woman, full of life, unconcerned and pretty despite the fact that she was ten years older than me. There was serenity in her and even now I could detect a lust for life.

'Yes, we would have been married despite the fact that I am so much older than you, but that wouldn't have mattered. We go much further back than that and no, we wouldn't have had children. I never got married, never found the right one, because he had already gone.'

Miss Jung, which in German also means 'young', now looked at me with a slightly sad yet somehow mischievous smile. I wondered whether the name she had given me was simply a metaphor for letting me know that when she was much younger she would have made an attractive partner for me.

At a stroke I was reminded of my real-life family with my beautiful wife, the love of my life, who had given us two beautiful daughters, and not a day had gone by when I had not felt our deep connection, despite the fact – or perhaps because of it – that we had such different natures.

Yet at this moment I looked at the wife who could have been, her blonde hair stylishly trimmed into a bob and an enticing smile which was full of earnest love. I felt attracted to her and deeply aware of a potentially consuming connection. This didn't escape her. She sipped her tea and looked at me out of the corners of her eyes.

'I never married,' she repeated. 'I always knew that any marriage would only ever be second best to what could have been.

There was always something missing when I met a man and this something was you.'

I felt left in a dilemma. She looked quite sad now, quite forlorn as she lowered her teacup and ran her finger round the rim of her cup, touching it comfortingly.

I too felt her sadness as if it was my own. I had rejected her despite never having met her in my life. I had chosen my wife and my two children and yet there was an element of guilt. But then I knew I had made the choice I did for the right reason. Had I not done so this lucid encounter on this other dimension would have been quite different.

It could have been the other way round. I could have married Miss Jung and never have met my wife and it could have been my wife Julia instead sitting here drinking tea in my lucid dream state, and her sad expression would have torn my heart apart and would have plunged me into inconsolable grief.

Meditation, 11:30 a.m.

The sun had finally burst through the clouds. I was also relieved that my foot was no longer hurting. I made a cup of tea and had a biscuit, then I settled down for meditation. For no other reason than variety I popped on my headphones in order to listen to my Om sound I had made up a while ago, which could induce a very deep state. Sometime this would conjure up strong hypnagogic images, which can be converted into entry points into the astral world.

The Ten Minute Moment

The moment I closed my eyes the sunlight burning through my closed eyelids conjured up colourful patterns. This was a good start to letting attentions play along with them and observing what would emerge. Sure enough, a few moments later I saw the fringes of open countryside appearing spontaneously. A lane leading into a village became bright and clear. It was important in such circumstances to allow the scene to emerge in a passive way simply by observing, uninvolved, without judging it or attempting to add or take anything away. Sometimes it decides to change on its own accord, but there is a moment where it becomes crystal clear and takes on a life of its own. It is then that I allow myself to be drawn into it. It is a practice which lets me abandon my position and enter the scene, fully conscious.

My country lane was basking in the height of summer noon light, hemmed in by luscious hedges, to the left a whitewashed cottage, very crisp and clean with sharp edges, but as I drew closer it faded away. Recalibrating my attention ended in a similar way. As I kept trying to make new connections, sleep finally gained the upper hand instead and I dropped into unconscious dreams.

I must have been gone for two hours. When I opened my eyes my head had sunk to my chest and my body was moulded firmly into my beanbag chair, having acquired its most natural position. My watch said 3 p.m. Looking out into the landscape it was cloudy, but the wind had dropped. Occasionally tears in the blanket of clouds appeared with glimpses of blue sky. Time to move my body. I decided to explore the gorge and the forest via a barely visible animal trail leading across my Sheilin to the back and up the hill.

The Ten Minute Moment

Living as I do now by the sea, nowhere near any woods, I only remember forests from my childhood and even then they were managed and maintained and nothing like the wilderness I found here. It was not a big forest at all but big enough not to be able to see beyond the trees. I followed a narrow path sitting precariously on the edge of a deep gorge with a stream splattering through it, occasionally via a small waterfall, and over millennia it had carved out its own territory, where the occasional tree had lost its foothold and had plunged down to form a bridge which nobody used. On the far side a steep granite cliff fell straight into it and on my side if I wanted to go down it would have been a steep grass and moss-covered descent, not to be undertaken lightly. Wherever I looked there were mighty fallen trees devoured by thick moss and huge firs reaching straight up clamouring for the sky, eager to grasp any available sunlight. From where I stood each direction formed a gothic archway of trees and each arch would have led me into a different world. At one end the roots of a fallen tree outlined the caricature of an ogre, with bare roots like knobbly hands, face and eyes and a black body fastened to the earth. There was no way past it.

However, I decided to stick to a small and very narrow path, which could have been formed by man or animal, carved by the considered wisdom of experience and knowledge of the dangers. Yet at its closest edge there was still a deep descent into the abyss and it reminded me of the fact that I was on my own; were I to trip and slip, nobody would probably find me, perhaps not for days, perhaps not ever.

These were of course the considerations of an urbanised mind, grossly exaggerated by an unfamiliar fear of hazards. It was still only four days into my adventure, and unsurprisingly my mind was not yet adapted to this strange alien planet. A person living life in this wilderness might equally wonder how on earth you would cross a busy road without risking your life.

Staring down into the abyss, then reaching for the camera, I knew that the photos would never adequately express the tingle I felt under my skin or the fastidious arrangement of my foothold to make sure I wouldn't slip as I was carefully selecting the right angle to get as close to the shot I wanted.

Soon I was more attracted by the gurgling sound of the water and the whispery echo and husky roar of the tall trees picking up the breeze with their crowns. I lowered my camera and listened transfixed like an animal might, perking its ears, listening out for a stalking predator. I relaxed when I became aware how beautifully the different sounds mingled and mixed and how the birds did their best to pitch their own musical notes to perfection among the trees and the branches. I was mesmerised; what harmony, what beauty, the voice of the forest. Never before had I been aware or would have remotely suspected that the forest had a voice like any other living thing.

As I hesitantly, silently urged forward, it had become indisputably clear to me that I had unwittingly stumbled into the inner sanctuary of an alien entity, the whole forest being a single creature. I looked at the sights, the thick moss covering the ground, absorbing my steps like green clouds without letting my feet know whether or when they would reach solid ground. I could easily have sunken into a bog or been devoured by an infinite space below it and never been any the wiser, such softness, such gentleness. There was no solid ground. My camera searched out the shadows the tall trees had cast over the soft mounts carpeted with moss and had painted their two-dimensional pattern over this multidimensional landscape.

So much more lay hidden beyond the grasp of the camera lens, which I could only perceive when I closed my eyes after following the sunbeams bobbing on the tall stems of the grass and perching on the tiny leaves of the abundant mosses. Behind my closed eyes, as I

5 – The Nine-Step Meditation towards Awakening

STRENGTH

Strength results from well-being. Strength is a manifestation of the pure light of consciousness. It is directly connected to it. Without strength the power of creation and this universe would not be possible. But I don't think of strength in terms like this. I simply pick up the word almost like a sound directly from a deeper part of my consciousness and open myself to it. I feel its power and energy. It is not my power and strength, it simply passes through me from its highest point of origin as an aspect of consciousness and its powerful light. I cannot influence it or bend it to my will, because it will not be weakened like this. I can only participate in strength and surrender to it and see where it will take me. I cannot get attached to strength because I am already strength when I surrender to this cosmic force.

I pick up this word three times like this and balance it in front and inside me, easily, without attachment, and then let it go.

rested against a tree, their remnant after-images began to tell a new story, gave me another version of the physical forest I had seen so far. Guided by the voice of the forest with its complex nuances of sounds a different reality emerged in my inner vision. The lights at the tip of the moss had reached down into its root where it formed filaments of light, a complex pattern of roots and veins, not random but following a symmetric order cast into fractal shapes, generating three-dimensional carpets in all directions within the earth and above the ground. In the air they were enhanced by tiny mosquitoes and fragments of pollen and dust, none of which claimed supremacy, but all adhering to a harmony which was an aspect of the whole. I saw moisture combining into tiny rootlike streams which saturated the ground and gathered at regular points where they made their way to the surface, nourishing the stream, all part of a gigantic tapestry, perfectly designed, which could be seen with inner eyes and heard with inner ears. I could see through the ground into the earth with my mind's eye.

When I opened my eyes I was blinded by the sun, which had chased the clouds wide open to grant me the view, triggered by its light. I was mesmerised and blessed to be handed such intimate views into nature's inner sanctuary. How little we perceive with our surface eyes and how much is revealed when we expand our vision to other levels.

I traced the small path up a hill until it emerged into the open. Here a different world appeared, a man-made one, with huge forests slaughtered, their trees harvested and ash-grey stumps remaining. The contrast was painful, so much so that it left me stunned and traumatised. I turned back, tracing my little path back through the wilderness, which had become so much a part of me. On my way home I pondered nature and man's lust to consume it for personal and economic gain.

Meditation, 7:00 p.m.

At seven I settled for my evening meditation, summing up the day with its huge adventures, some in a parallel world, some in the woods and underground. Even around my little Sheilin temple the universe is a vast playing field. There was stillness, the day had been laid to rest and I was listening to the dusk. No wind, no movement, nature in contemplative mood slowly settling into the evening.

Day five, Tuesday 4 June
The Terrifying Face of God

Meditation, 5 a.m.

Strange, it was only now, after three full days and passing the halfway point of my retreat, that my silent companion gently made its presence felt again. Until now, despite all the meditation, the peace and the enchanting surroundings, I had been too intoxicated to pay any attention to its presence. My silent companion is an awareness of some kind of presence in my life, a personification of stillness, the present of the moment personified which allows me to relate to it almost as if it was another person on a personal and intimate level.

However, this silent presence has no name and never communicates with words. Every question I pose it answers with silence, but a silence offering an infinite space, an unfathomable depth of wisdom from which I can scoop my answers intuitively. My silent companion is very mindful of my freedom and will never

impose anything on me. One may wonder what use such a companion is. My answer would be that if we were to personify the silent companion and assimilate its characteristic our world would be transformed overnight. Imagine having a partner who always loves you, disregards your faults and afflictions, who gives you the space and the freedom to unfold, develop your potential and to reflect and arrive at your own conclusions. One who never imposes him/herself on you, makes no demands, but does not allow illusion to get hold of you. One who does not judge you and gives you the freedom to make errors in order for you to learn and progress, and supports you with wisdom to restore order. One who will forgive you instantly and clearly shows you where you went wrong with love so that you can learn and progress. A companion who never deserts you and is at hand at a moment's notice, loving and caring, who steps aside should you wrong others and lets you realise your mistake, while watching lovingly over events unfolding as a result, showing you the love you need to untie life's knots. How can such a partner not be a good companion?

My silent companion is subtle and gentle. It does not speak and only communicates with silence. In its presence I feel like a child at play watched over by its parent. Instead of feeling observed, I feel safe and secure, supported in the gentlest of ways, but never see it in any way as intrusive. It is fragile and subtle like a butterfly which retreats the moment I try to capture it with my thoughts or if I try to focus my attention on it too directly. It only settles on me when my heart is still and then it dispenses a nourishing stream of silent joys, which have no equivalent in ordinary life. It pops up during the day and points my attention to a father doting on his child or how the light draws designs on the pavement or the raindrops making patterns on the water, and every time it shares these occasions it showers me with joy. It is never far away either, because it is in every object, always forming the background wherever I go. It makes me feel as if the world outside is the extension of my living room and wherever I go I feel safe because I am on home ground. To connect to it all I have to do is open my eyes and pick out any object at random and just note its existence. The world is proof that it exists and it proves it every moment. I don't need belief or faith, I just need to look and see. I can see that it forms the very essence of everything that is. Now, sitting here in my little Sheilin, looking through the open door into its magnificent creation, I gratefully acknowledge its presence and feel its warmth surrounding me and entering my body.

The Ten Minute Moment

Since last night the wind had fallen and come to a complete stop. Gazing through the open door into the valley not a leaf was stirring. In my normal life back home by the seaside this in itself would be a novelty. I could only hear the distant white noise of the stream making its way down from the mountain and the birdsong without the accompaniment of rustling leaves.

At home the stillness meditation has been my daily bread, the one I have been most fond of, found most natural, requiring no intent other than being still. It was here where I came closest to my silent companion, connecting with my heart and quietly acknowledging its presence. Now I noticed it had already been waiting for me patiently, and when I looked at the mountain at the far end of the valley it was there too, had been there before it became the mountain and before that when this land was formed. All the time it had never wavered, never taken leave, patiently observing all changes. Now it was sitting silently with me in meditation, sharing its abundant peace.

Three hours later I was forced to put sunflower seeds out on the veranda by a group of little birds reproachingly hopping along on their plasticky little feet, drumming cutely on the wooden boards of the veranda, going as far as daringly perching on my threshold, staring sideways at me, blatantly demanding their dues. They only took advantage of a small window of opportunity until Tails arrived, of course, who was quite unaware of his superior status and went straight to work in his eating. A day before he had quietly introduced me to his mate, who had joined him to sample the cuisine, but quickly disappeared again. I was still trying to figure out

The Ten Minute Moment

the unique characteristics which distinguished him from his other friend or soulmate. I decided that the tufts on his ears might be slightly longer, but now he was working himself through the first row of sunflower kernels and was eyeing up the next row of pumpkin seeds while still completing the first.

I began noticing my fondness for this creature, admiring his efficiency, the way he used his tiny hands and the rapid snapping of his little jaw, grinding the seeds. The way he changed position, looking adorable from any angle. As I love-bombed the little fellow with affection the birds arrived on the scene, stealing little kernels from under his nose and flying off, landing again and stealing.

Half an hour later the veranda was cleared, my visitors gone. Without changing position I closed my eyes and sank into a deep, intangible peace.

Meditation, 8 a.m.

Meditation can be many things. I have never allowed rigid systems to interfere with my freedom to find a pathway to penetrate into the deepest, most intimate secrets of my inner self and higher nature once I had learned to be in charge of my mind and its thoughts. This freedom began a long time ago the moment I had silenced the inner commentator.

I had sunk into my beanbag seat and begun to focus naturally and automatically on the unmissable birdsong and I knew this would become my birdsong meditation. After a few minutes my attention was pinned on every note they sang, whichever direction their hypnotic sounds were coming from. After a while it became quite clear to me that they didn't seem to sing in isolation to assert their tiny little bird egos. No, they were singing not as isolated entities but in harmony, responding dynamically to each other's notes.

With my inner vision held suspended in the dark void within, my ears methodically collected all sounds as if they were pearls found on an exotic beach. As I gathered their treasure they found themselves strung on a colourful necklace stretching across the inner void. I began to notice that connected to each note was a colour and to each sound bite a pattern, and when one bird began to sing it released a pattern of colours into the void where I saw it drifting like a pretty tapestry towards the birds at the far end of the hill below me. The moment it arrived, which was in an instant, it was picked up by other birds who in turn wove their own unique sound pattern with colour and design and posted it back towards the other birds. Within no time the dark space of the void was filled with a variety of fractal tapestries which were an artwork of astounding beauty and complexity. Not a note was out of place or in any way random. The little feathered fellows knew how to communicate and how to talk to each other in a way that would put ordinary human conversation to shame.

Before long I was reading their songs with its changing pattern like a picture book some celestial artist may have drawn and was now submitting to the publisher. There was no duplication and even if they used repeating melodies they only enforced the magnificent rhythm of the tapestry which now began to stretch right across my inner space. I succumbed and then surrendered to their hypnotic beauty and the incredible scale of this artwork of sound. Nothing was out of synch, the fractals changing dynamically to the communication, evolving new designs, on higher frequencies, then allowing it to fall and disintegrate into droplets of colour, then beginning anew on a different theme. Even when a completely new sound entered the landscape, it instantly found its part in this magnificent new web. Not a single sound was out of place, not a single note ignored.

When I opened my eyes, returning from this new and fascinating world to settle back into my old ways on my familiar planet, an hour had passed and I wondered whether just by listening without thought I might have decoded involuntarily the secret of birdsong.

I had tea, cherishing every sip, my eyes closed, relishing the after-effect of my journey into bird paradise, which now had taken leave; it was the tea warming me on the inside which now became the priority of my attention. I felt a deep gratitude for what I had received. I was grateful for the tea which had such a warming, invigorating effect.

Gratitude is always good, never wasted. It is good to start a day with gratitude and appreciation. Everything else follows naturally from there. As I finished my tea my gratitude still lingered, wafted out of my cabin and settled like a soft blanket over the valley before me, saying 'thank you' to the scenery. The valley returned the compliment by revealing its morning splendour. I was blessed and honoured by its beauty and when I closed my eyes for the next meditation, love had taken its place, powerful love, seamlessly evolving from my gratitude, rising from my chest.

Love has its own energy and if it is powerful enough it can take us on a long journey into wondrous lands, into territories we may never have dreamed of. There is a good reason for the saying 'Let love be your guide'.

Love has no ego, no sense of self. Love only knows of giving. On this wave of love rising from my heart I took leave from the world. It was love untethered, in its purest and most sublime form, taking on its own shape and pattern like the birdsong. When love is released it offers joy, great joy, which in itself has its own wave forms of expression, emotions which transcend the self and can best be used in fanning love further until it rises as a luminous sun compelling everything into its orbit.

The sun of love had now become the object of my meditation. The only way to focus on it was to surrender to it. Love can never be divided. To fully understand and appreciate love I had to become love, and surrendering to it was the only way. The moment I did it ceased to be a sun and became a stream, rising into the air and then cascading down in its blessing, taking me with it. Now star-littered and strong, a river of light, it shimmered in sublime colours as it tumbled through the void and there was nothing to stop it. At every turn it revealed new patterns, new emanation of its infinite potential, its unrestricted and beautified expression, until it found its way back to its own source. Everything it encountered on its path was consumed by it and left enriched, invigorated with new life. It cared not in the least whether anything it met was antagonistic or even opposed to it. To love, everything was equally worthy to be embraced because nothing could ever lessen it. It took its nature directly from its source and knew that everything it encountered was at its primal source made of love. Riding the stream, surrendering my all to its impulse, I rose and rose, exhilarated by its power into pure joy and ecstasy.

As I slowly opened my eyes and sized up my surroundings, my body had become part of the furniture. I could still perceive the external world through my eyes, but my body had turned into a shell, a cardboard cutout. I watched in astonishment as layer upon layer of what I thought had been reality was being stripped away before my very eyes.

6 – The Nine-Step Meditation towards Awakening

ABUNDANCE

With strength comes abundance. Abundance is everywhere because nothing can exist without the powerful light of consciousness; consciousness creates abundance and wherever I look I see it. Abundance does not skimp. Abundance is a quality of the heart which never exhausts itself. The more it gives, the more abundance it receives. I can observe abundance everywhere, because it is so closely related to the manifesting light of consciousness. All I need to do is surrender my heart to abundance and I will find it everywhere.

Again, I just pick up the word 'abundance' before it even forms into an idea or a concept, suspend it lightly in front of me three times and let it go naturally.

The Ten Minute Moment

What was that thing which had vacated my body? Yes, it was still love, opening and shutting my eyelids, manoeuvring my body. Love interpenetrated and transcended all dimensions. But what was love? The moment I posed the question I felt a powerful surge in my heart. All consuming, it showed no concern for words or explanation, was not interested in answers only in action. It was an extraordinary stream of bountiful light, surging forward, spreading out with only one purpose, to bestow its treasure indiscriminately on everything it encountered. I was riding its surge when suddenly something unexpected happened. Love had returned to itself. Love had ceased and in its place was a void, a void with a presence.

Everything stopped. A faint residue hung in the space around me like the remaining embers of fireworks gently drifting through the air, featherlike, before touching the ground. The surge of energy had calmed abruptly and was absorbed by its own impulse, which left a momentous stillness in its place. A stillness which was simply the root of all motion that had gone on before.

I could no longer be sure of what was happening. It was beyond and outside anything I had come to know and understand. It was totally new, something without precedence. My body began to mobilise to account for what was taking place, but it failed. The stillness was too vast in its scope to be grasped. With my eyes open I no longer recognised the reality in front of me as anything I was familiar with. This was not reality as I knew it, the familiar turf of old. This was something completely new and totally different. The thing was, it had always been different, but I hadn't noticed. It was reality with a monumental presence and truth, stripped of any familiarity. It was radical and so remorselessly real in that, that it made me simply shudder. I could almost not bear it and I cringed under the burden to consider that anything I had experienced in the past and I had held to be real was no longer authentic. It revolutionised everything and put everything that went before into question. It was almost too big to handle and for a moment I wanted to go back and hide, shouting, 'No, please, let me be small again, unburdened by its awesome implications, so I can crawl away and hide in the dark corners of the illusions which were so familiar to me.' But there was no hiding, no turning back. 'You asked for it, now deal with it,' it seemed to say. And every moment I confronted and faced it, it became more overwhelming, more clear, sharper, irrefutable, irreversible and finally irresistible, the truth, the whole of it, the reality of it.

For a split moment I considered the concept of 'God', but the implications were too enormous. How could I even touch it, hold it even for a second? But it didn't go away. It presented itself in its terrifying awesomeness, a reality which unrolled and unfolded, unravelling its awesome depth, and I was sitting and staring at the ground in front of me, which had opened into an infinite abyss of unmanifested possibilities, wondering what that thing was that was terrifying me into oblivion and the other 'thing' that was terrified.

In an instant I recognised that I was just a thought, an imagination with no substance whatsoever. For whatever reason I had imagined myself to exist, leading an independent life. To carry it off I had assumed a disguise, a shell, which I pretended to be 'I'. Now the deception was unmasked, laid bare for all to see. I could instantly see why I was hiding under my disguises. The truth was too terrifying, too massive, with nothing to cling on to or to grasp. The terrifying face of God was threatening to consume, to obliterate its own thought, me.

I had died many deaths before. The most common form is physical death, which doesn't change anything, only the flesh dies but we emerge the same and intact on the other side. But then there is a second death which is not often spoken about. It is the death of our ego, the demise of our social and personal identification. This death occurs when we surrender all our attachments and identifications. Then, relieved of all emotional baggage, we are free to enter the proverbial paradise or heaven, much talked about in all religions. This is a place which knows no negativity, no suffering, where all our most positive dreams become instant reality, realised to a degree which makes everything experienced on the physical level a pale shadow of this new reality.

This, however, was the death of all death, the ultimate annihilation. This was the third kind of death, which put into question my own creation and hence it became incomprehensible in the extreme. If everything has been surrendered what is there left to be terrified of? What was this monstrosity that was threatening to devour me and send my consciousness into utter oblivion and annihilation?

I had arrived at the zero point. The only thing at this point of naught still there was no more than an impulse, a vague attitude set in motion to comprehend, to understand and discover its own impulse. It was an atom of need, an illusion of being a separate item. But to understand it had to pass the zero point, the unfathomable gulf that waited underneath. The great uncertainty of what would happen if I passed this singularity became unbearable, this single thought which insisted to be me, which had been equipped with random substance and nurtured as a separate unit sent out through the aeons of time to be born and transformed, to explore its own mystery in the process, wondering what it was, searching for meaning and believing it was real.

What I had become was an atom of need, used as a tool for an unknown operator to focus and explore and which had slowly evolved and come to reside over a kingdom of knowledge with vistas of suffering and paradises to claim for itself. It had now arrived at the point of its own origin, had outlived its usefulness and was about to be surrendered and reabsorbed into its source, pulverised and annihilated with nothing at all left of it, not even a record that it ever existed. Over many lifetimes it had been given carte blanche, seduced by its own grandeur, importance and significance. And even much later in its career it may no longer have seen itself as separate from consciousness, yet it could still take comfort in the fact that it was an intrinsic part of it, an instrument of knowledge which had a mind that could experience, a role created for a purpose; and now it had become redundant. It was time for its final dissolution, the moment of its absolute truth, to cease to exist. This atom of need was I. I, a divine thought with a purpose and an imbedded quintessence. Could it be that I was God, the all merciful, or was this just an assumption, a desperate grasp to hang on to existence?

The zero point was reached. All was now put into question. One more step and there would be no return. This was the extent of the abyss I was staring into, the merciless face of God.

In my youth I had heard about Kali, the Hindu goddess of destruction, and Shiva, the destroyer of worlds. Until now they had never made sense to me. God always stood for good, I thought, but now I saw the truth and the Hindu gods' true terrifying aspects became clear. Just beneath this terrifying perception lay blandly the stark reality behind all existence, the destroyer of worlds, an energy more powerful than all created universes combined, a monstrous powerhouse, brighter and more forceful than the light of all the billions of suns and galaxies combined which had sprung from its source. And here I sat about to witness my own origin and my ultimate and final disintegration without any prospect of returning to anything that I would recognise as me, myself.

Surely all my life this was what I had aimed for, was it not? The ultimate, the truth, the final resolution? Was this not what all the saints and sages had been preaching? Or had I been seduced by poetry and prose? At this very moment, rather than submitting and rejoicing, I found myself praying to be spared.

It is not my time, please let me go!

I closed my eyes and resisted the terrifying storm which started to engulf me, tearing at me and ripping me apart, while I started to expand into terrifying dimensions. I despairingly started to cling to any idea or any thought I could get hold of, resisting the violent onslaught, and slowly and mercifully the energy relented and dissipated. I rode out the storm. 'I', whatever that was, had been spared. I had won.

'I' had been saved. 'I' had won over annihilation, from being destroyed for all eternity. I had triumphantly defied absorption into an ultimate reality without a trace of me being left. I had been spared to see another day and been granted asylum by an old and so familiar world.

As I clung on to the extremely shaky home of the asylum seeker, clutching on to its porous walls for dear life, still shaking, thankfully a veil descended over the world around me, a merciful stupor. Many things had already been lost in the struggle and I became thankful for the token bits of territory I once more began to

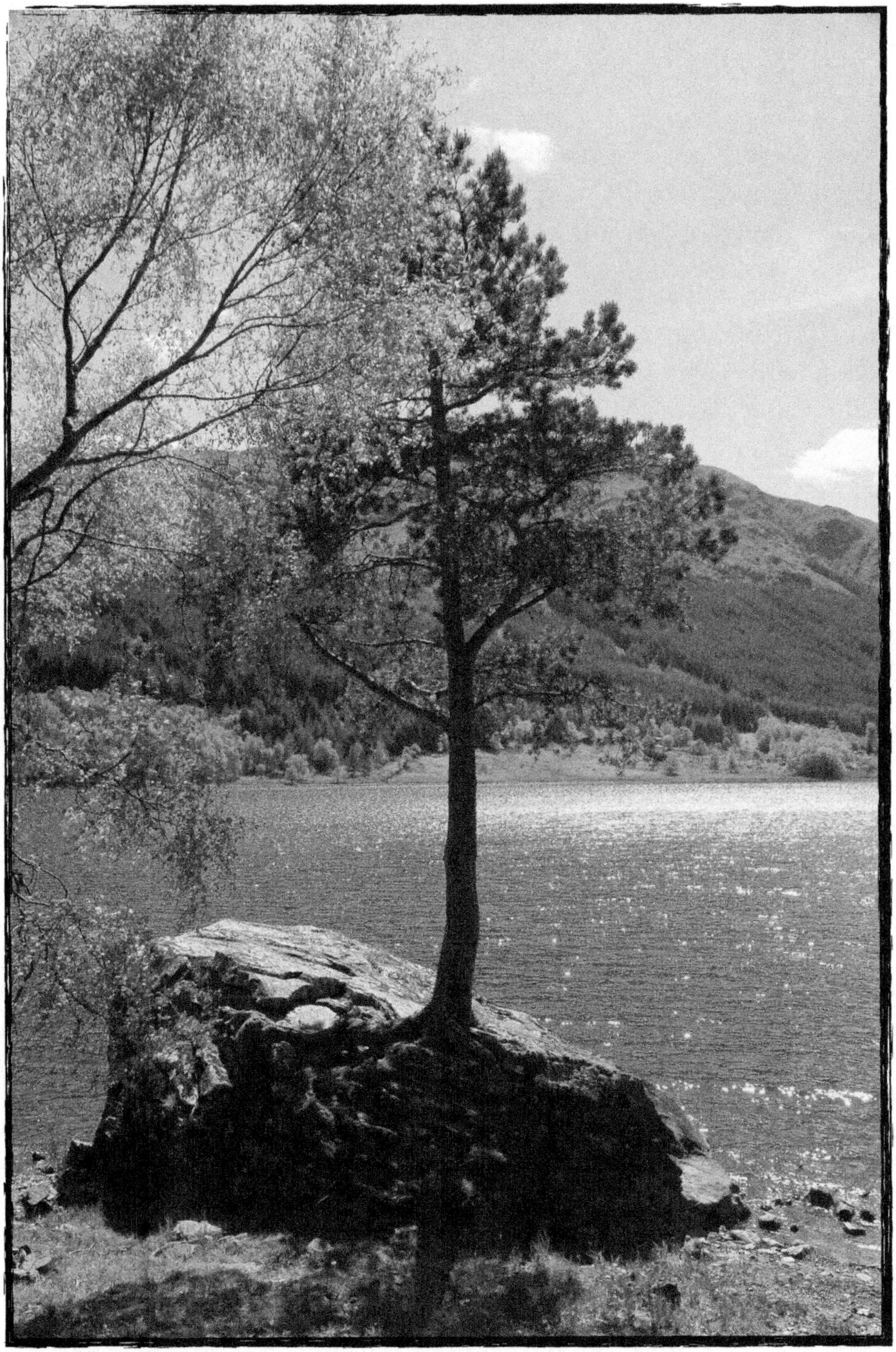

recognise as familiar ground. I began to set foot again in the gluey yet merciful comfort of being something, even if it had no name yet and no thought.

The terrifying reality of the unspeakable had been conquered. I felt a soothing goodness around me, which had been handed to me like a warming coat, like somebody who had been snatched back to safety from the torrents of a mighty river. Now I felt safe again and curiously peaceful. My silent companion had taken pity on me, had shown me its mercy. It had stood by, not asked to be involved in what I was experiencing, not forcing me to take the final step. It was here, all merciful, handing me back my illusion.

I had approached the fierce inferno of God without humility and hence without protection. I had stumbled like a child into a forest fire, seduced by the bright light. I had looked at reality wondering what it was made of and had almost plunged into its abyss, unprotected, but there was silence now and a comforting peace. I had returned safely into my wilderness, watched over by my silent companion and finding its comfort.

Lunch, 1 p.m.

I had a shower and a change of clothing. Somehow I felt purified, forgiven. For years and years I had conditioned myself to leave everything behind, like a warrior preparing for battle not knowing when or whether he would return. That had been the plan, taken from books and practised in countless meditations. I had trained myself to leave anything behind at a moment's notice. Sure, it now allowed me to no longer feel attached to my failure and I humbly accepted that I had simply been unprepared to face the truth in its ultimate essence.

After I dressed I decided to have an elaborate crunchy peanut butter and jam sandwich, which I cut in half and placed on a white porcelain plate. I cut the last banana in half and served it as a pudding. I greatly cherished the modest pleasure it provided. I also made a cup of tea which I placed together with the sandwich on a little round table I had stolen from my bedside and parked on the veranda. On my little wooden chair outside I propped up three cushions, two for the base and one for the back. With my legs up high anchored on the banister my body felt soothed and my mind and soul compensated for the prospect of total destruction.

While chewing my lunch I chewed over why I hadn't sought the protection of my silent companion to guide me across the abyss. Isn't that why the ancient scriptures always state that you need a guide to cross the void, a master, an enlightened teacher? Here I was in the presence of my silent companion and yet not for a moment had I considered surrendering to it and enlisting its help.

And while serving my body with food I still pondered my cowardice, the missed opportunity to enter my ultimate reality, the heart of God. I had made a mockery of my lifelong quest to unite with my innermost origin. I had failed.

To console myself I was quick to question whether the many people who so casually talked of God really had any idea of what it was they so flippantly talked about. I could no longer believe them, their banal-sounding claims, their understated mentioning of the word 'God'. All my life I had been anxious to avoid the word, perhaps feeling instinctively that it was a word too big to utter and that what it represented was too massive to handle. Now I knew why. When I heard people speak of God's will, God's word and what God wants from us and what his plan and intentions were I felt positively uncomfortable. Would anybody dare to mention its name had they come as close to seeing its terrifying face?

Where was the love of God so often talked about? I quickly realised that without love, such love was not forthcoming. Why had love deserted me at the moment of truth? What was it that I hadn't grasped? For a whole hour I indulged in thoughts until they began to fizzle out like a raincloud having dispersed its water, and what I was left with was like the cloud devoid of its content, a bank of mist which had little reality and very little clarity and was now drifting aimlessly and pointlessly over a vast stretch of land which barely acknowledged the clouds passing over them. I had re-entered the fog of human consciousness with all its limitations.

The Ten Minute Moment

Exploration, 2 p.m.

By 2 p.m. I was a complete bag of flesh again and turned affectionately towards my camera, my external inner eye. I had reassembled a sense of purpose, a reason to live. As I took the camera apart, trying various lenses, I relished the guilty pleasure of the escape these simple peripherals offered. They gave me a new reason to exist, and how merciful to be allowed such indulgence and be provided with new meaning.

A camera eye makes life simple again. As I look through the viewfinder I focus my attention, narrow it down until an image emerges with a story to convey. I had a reason to be alive again. I had a story to tell, a never-ending story. 'Thank you, God, for sparing me from making the ultimate sacrifice.'

So I made my way down to the lake, where the water had eroded the shore, with trees and roots hanging precariously over the edge, the soil washed away from underneath sentencing the trees above them to a slow death. It was here that I began to discover a new world, a close-up world of a drawn-out death.

The camera knows nothing about its relative position in space. It relies on me and my direction and I in turn rely on the director within my heart. I only see what my heart wants to see. Soon I discovered the fractal network of the roots, the trees with their branches. Here, too, God and nature had made a point, had thrown into focus a woven pattern, a physical thought and a very visual one at that, which I began to read in the same way I had unravelled the birdsong in the morning. Any thoughts I made about myself were woven into similar patterns, my own existence patterns of lifetime after lifetime without an end in sight, just me as an endless, reconfigured creation.

Two hours later I made my way back up the hill again towards my Sheilin temple. The exercise and the sun had re-established the balance between body and spirit. To top it up I had a cup of jasmine tea and a rice cake with honey. The birds and squirrel too had long finished their pickings and it was time to treat them to a few more seeds.

Meditation, 4 p.m.

Now it was time to be quiet again. I still felt somehow shaken when thinking back to my encounter of the morning. Things weren't quite

7 – The Nine-Step Meditation towards Awakening

WISDOM

With abundance comes wisdom. Wisdom reveals the deep unfathomable knowingness of the pure consciousness. Wisdom is not a result of my thoughts, my cognitive abilities or the head. Wisdom results from the knowing heart. It is knowing instead of thinking. Thought has nothing to do with it. Wisdom already knows and it is not a process to be arrived at. Wisdom lies at the root of creation. Without wisdom the universe would not function the way it functions. Wisdom is at work in all that is happening. There is even wisdom in the existence of ignorance. I don't have to concern myself in finding wisdom. Wisdom will find me when I surrender to the pure light of consciousness.

Again I pick up this word and let it unfold and reveal itself without my interference, lightly and easily, three times and then let it go.

normal. Something had shifted. Something epic and powerful. The ground underneath my feet no longer felt as solid as before. Precarious cracks had appeared in the world I was in, ready to shift at any moment and to come tumbling down, perhaps to bury me alive. In front of me was still the imprint of an abyss which was barely covered by the thin veil of ordinary perception.

Relatively speaking, though, I felt quite safe again. Safe enough to notice a strange thrill from a safe enough distance, a 'what if' thrill and a reckless temptation of wanting to go back, but it was just a thought, and perhaps not even up to me. The moment had passed. Something else had been exposed in the abyss and I knew that it would not let me rest. From my safe distance it looked and felt like a seam of gold, a prospector's dream, but it too was only a thought, a feeling which didn't consider the awesome reality.

My meditation did not go too well. I had too many thoughts and they left me exhausted. I yearned for more trivial ones, thoughts spun by children which would tumble into my mind with their innocent play, as if they had been let loose on the first day of the summer holiday. And thankfully they came, thoughts of the birds picking their seeds which I could hear tapping on the veranda, and what had happened to Tails, my red squirrel? I decided to let simple thoughts have their fun as I lay down on the bed, relishing the heaviness of my body and limbs. There were other pleasant thoughts, weaving their innocent yarn, undisturbed and free to talk. Soon they took on a life of their own by spinning their threads into innocent dreams.

The Ten Minute Moment

At 7 p.m. I managed a two-hour stillness meditation, after which I settled down on the veranda with my feet up, watching the clouds and the shadows climbing up the mountain, the colours muting and the sounds settling down to rest. Even the stream seemed to have acquired an aspect of stillness. I turned in at eleven.

Day six, Wednesday 5 June
The Ten Minute Moment

Dreaming, 5 a.m.

In my last dream, before I woke up, I had been occupying a luxurious penthouse, the top floor of a tall building right in the centre of a big city. From up here I was looking onto the forest of human dwellings. The roof of my penthouse slid open to expose the whole interior to the world outside, turning the blue sky above into my ceiling. The symbolism was quite obvious to me. I had always seen buildings as representing myself. In this dream the building had become much taller than the one I had dreamed about at the outset of my journey when I arrived here. Then there was Andy the pregnant foreman – myself – in charge of the renovation project. Here, not only had the modest, unrenovated building project transformed into a tall multi-storey house, I also occupied the penthouse overlooking the world, and with the roof removed the sky was the limit.

I concluded that my experience the previous day might have been instrumental in removing the roof and with it my limitation. This thought excited me. Perhaps the experience had been enough to have shifted obstacles in my path.

I noticed another strange analogy to my life here in the wild, looking out across the valley to the forest of trees opposite and below me. In our cities the human forest leaves nothing to nature. Everything is conceived, thought of, planned, manufactured and fabricated. From beginning to end everything we see in our cities is processed through the mind, millions of minds, and yet it follows a similar fractal pattern to nature with its arteries of roads, the pumping life blood of traffic, the rivers of human lives streaming like water through the passages, over pavements, crossing roads to converge on centres of habitation, manufacture, food production and consumption as well as entertainment. We are not that much different from the bees, the ants or the birds in their illustrious swarms, though we imagine we are, a somewhat self-elected species to put ourselves above the rest of creation. In reality we are simply another chosen stream for consciousness to explore. There is a plan and wisdom to how nature executes and governs our lives and how we, motivated by creating a paradise on earth, instinctively follow a blueprint laid out within a deeper level of our being. Down here, unknown to us, we follow the fractal designs from the higher planes of consciousness, tuning and refining them until they take us close back to its original source.

The dream of the penthouse with its elevated view of the human forest showed me the close connection to my Sheilin 'penthouse' up in the mountains looking down on the forest and nature below. I also saw the distance we had come, rising from our close proximity to nature into our current world.

As I contemplated these ideas from a new height I sank into a deep, thought-free and wholesome trance state with images rising up from deep below, which I could not immediately identify and over which I seemed to have no control. They led me into a much deeper level of my meditation until I arrived at some kind of blueprint for our human species. I had risen to the top of a metaphorical building and began viewing the world from a future probability perspective with astonishing clarity.

Laid out in front of me was a future world. I could see completely new technologies fully applied, where houses and dwellings are grown organically from artificial DNA controlled by thought, which in turn is controlled by an adopted process of a self-regulating ecosystem. Mankind has internalised the mechanics and wisdom of ecosystems which consider the world as a whole, allowing nature and man to prosper in equal measure, living in balance side by side. Food and goods are produced by thought-induced processes operating on a quantum level using revolutionary new technologies which no longer rely on monstrous production plants and power stations for energy. The economy of wealth is replaced by an economy of need, which equally addresses all aspects of needs, from physical and emotional to cultural and spiritual ones across the whole spectrum of our species and the whole of life on our planet.

Out of curiosity I focused on more detail. The science of the future is tied to quantum processing, evolving new processes and solutions in the blink of an eye. It will employ fractal algorithms for the production of goods. Industrial complexes will be replaced by energy being produced locally simply from the light and the air surrounding us; it will be stored and released efficiently. Cloth will be grown dynamically, its texture manipulated by thought. Food supply will be abundant and consumption regulated by the need of the body. Health issues are mostly a thing of the past. We will be able to address any problems before they arise. Most people will be able to choose the time and manner of their transition which they have already mapped out before they die, but it is not a brave new world, there is freedom of choice. We will have learned how to communicate with our departed friends and family as easily as using a phone. It is widely accepted that life is a dynamic process rooted in the perception of its here and now, thus allowing us spontaneous access to its treasures.

I saw technologies in action where our dreams can be accessed and manipulated into lucid dreams, creating whole virtual worlds which will allow us to train ourselves in parallel in skills previously unimaginable. Science will be conducted from higher dimensional levels applying completely new methods of research. People will be able to participate in each other's lives and understand them in virtual simulations. Needs, which may have been neglected or overlooked in early childhood or arise out of a deep inner drive, can be addressed and compensated in an immersive virtual way. Crime is virtually impossible because of instant feedback of consequences which serve as a deterrent, and an all-too-obvious awareness of our connectedness within a whole system of consciousness. People will be able to share on an experiential level and it is understood that man's existence is taking place simultaneously on multiple dimensions. We will no longer perceive ourselves as separate entities divorced and alienated from each other by our physical bodies, but instead experience ourselves within society as units of the same core consciousness, working in harmony for our common good. Our learning is accelerated and the main energy for creation is powered and motivated by the heart, with the rewards distributed to all life. We will have learned that our intelligence is no longer perceived as being determined by the brain, but that each cell in our body provides an access point into a greater consciousness. We are a divine species just evolving from the darkness of our ignorance.

The Ten Minute Moment

We are not there yet, but we are well on our way. I rose higher still in my meditation into the far-flung realms of our futures to learn of an angelic species, man, connected to all life, beautiful and perfect, sustained by love and created to express the highest principles of its creation. I began to understand the secret plan behind our evolution as a species from our first split from the animal kingdom to our exalted unification with the source of our very creation.

The visions vanished. My silent companion gently reminded me of what was real and what was merely a possible timeline of the future. What was real was its presence, which I simply could not ignore, and it was my heart which forged the link. Though when I became more aware of the sounds of nature flooding in from the outside I simultaneously knew that the silent companion was much larger than a presence felt in my chest. It was also the outside. Where is the limit of that which simply is?

I rested in this and after an hour I could simply see the world of the silent companion outside my Sheilin through my closed eyelids as if my body no longer existed as a shield.

Being able to see through closed eyelids is not a rare meditation phenomenon and it indicates a shift of consciousness from the physical into the subtle body. It is an experience which in the past has enabled me, by applying a little bit more focus, to leave my body, gliding out into the open like a large bird, riding effortlessly on the wings of consciousness where I can fly out and rise above the clouds, leaving the earth far behind, climbing into the sky until its blue fades into the black of outer space, and from there it is left to my imagination where it will take me. At times I could simply think of a member of my family, those still alive and those no longer with us, and pay them a visit, embrace and chat to them as if they were physically right next to me. I had done so on many occasions. But this was different, it simply informed me that perception is not limited to the physical senses. Any thought of going anywhere had no relevance now other than being a distraction. What I witnessed now was of far deeper significance.

The stillness, gently and with the greatest kindness imaginable, began to disperse its blessing, a gentle, embalming benediction. With my eyes still closed it felt as if the ceiling of my skull became illuminated, my brain no longer an organ of functioning molecules and cells, but more like a giant light bulb. My heart was touched reassuringly by my silent companion, which proved its presence with its benediction, raining down on me like droplets of light, prompting my heartfelt surrender. I relished it, whirled within and scattered simultaneously into atoms of deep joy, cascading through my own body via luminous streams of light. Here I remained, without thought, sat motionless, observed, quietly, in stillness . . . I am.

When I opened my eyes two hours had gone by. Before me, through the valley, at the bottom of my Sheilin temple, I saw the lake. It had turned into a mirror. Not a single wave, not a breath of air, not one leaf was stirring and not a single blade of grass was even gently swaying in the wind.

I had stopped the world. Not I, the person sitting here in meditation, because that was no longer 'I' but a much greater me that was out there stretching from horizon to horizon, having been there long before my body existed and long, long before that, encompassing the world every moment without fail. I accepted it calmly as the way it was and is.

The thing which had the appearance of a human body and was little more than a thought, an aspect of creation, was left sitting in its beanbag chair but not excluded. It too was 'I', sanctified and elevated, lit up and left with the knowledge that if it rose to its feet and walked across the hill not a blade of grass would bend under its weight or its step and the air around it would not be moved by its breath. There was no 'I' occupying the body that thought of itself as a separate object.

I knew this was a special day, a day like no other.

Camera meditation, 8:30 am

The squirrel and the birds had picked up all the seeds I had laid out for their breakfast. Now it was time to cater for my own body.

After a simple breakfast with tea and one slice of toast I felt impelled to go to the placid lake and examine its mirror surface with my camera.

Mirrors are powerful archetypes. In my dreams I enter into a mirror image of my physical world, though the mirror image is not an exact copy, only an approximation. Here too the mirror image created by the placid lake is only a reflection, not even perfect. There are objects caught on its skin and ever so subtly a breath of wind sneaks in and disturbs the surface at certain points. Neither the world nor its mirror image are perfect, because if they were no movement would be possible. Creation would end and there would be nowhere to go. Its perfection is its imperfection.

As I cruised with the camera pinned to my eye I observed another aspect of the mirror surface, which was the symmetry it created between the shoreline and its reflection. This is a symmetry I recognise from the root of my mind. I feel a strong attraction to symmetry, its kaleidoscopes of shapes and pattern bubbling in infinite variations through the higher realms of imagination, in a realm of thought which can no longer think in pictures because it still assembles the means to create the pictures. Symmetry is at the root of all and when I find stillness symmetry enters my mind and is reflected in my world. The mirror of the lake offered a similar attraction, revealing the principle on a massive scale. And there I was, standing in the middle of a giant kaleidoscope, witnessing it in my body.

Now skirting the pebbled shore I saw symmetry and pattern emerging from everywhere. My mind was restoring everything back to its original order. By taking pictures I was tracing the world back to its primal state, back to symmetry and order.

I kept walking and taking pictures along the shoreline, pointing the camera into washed-out caves, twisting and creeping through undergrowth, dodging fallen trees and sliding on the mud. I was an animal again, in harmony and opposition to its world. How exciting this felt. I was also a hunter, a stalker of images, gathering supplies to sustain the spirit.

Back in my little temple I made a cup of tea, probably the last one as I saw and smelled the warning signs of the milk going off. It would have to be herbal from now on.

Stillness meditation, 12:30 p.m.

Fifteen minutes into my meditation it started to rain. I could hear a stereophonic white noise entering my cabin. Slowly the rain revealed its more subtle nuances, a melodious sound from droplets hitting leaves, the wooden steps outside my door and the roof. As I opened my eyes I saw a soft grey curtain being drawn across the valley between me and the mountain opposite. The birdsong had stopped too. Their fractal concert abandoned, they had been caught by surprise, their beautiful tapestry of sound surrendered to the water falling from the sky.

I closed my eyes and again fell back and surrendered to the silence, which surrounded me whether my eyes were open or shut. The rain had been delivered without wind and with my eyes closed I could feel its droplets made of light, not of water. Stillness is not a void where nothing happens. Stillness is the impartial observer of the happening.

My eyes fleetingly scanned the landscape. The lake had become calm again like the mirror. The trees listened silently for the wind, which can only be seen in the distance, swaying the fluffy clouds, gently persuading them to dispense their load over the hilltops.

The sun was hidden. Grey had its own nobility, muting the colours, ushering them into less extravagant hues. All the shades of green of the trees were huddled together, held aloft on dark stalks of twigs and branches against the silver clouds. The light appeared to carry the ambient sound from the stream, protected by the trees across the gorge towards my hut. The mist across the valley was muting the mountain, holding it in check so as not to overwhelm the subtle yet sombre foliage of the birches and the elms. Nature was showing its restraint and yet its awesome presence.

Meditation, 4 p.m.

As is only too obvious in an environment like this, the eyes don't easily stay shut during meditation. When I closed my eyes all that I saw was the black canvas of my eyelids, but with my eyes open I could see out through the door of my Sheilin temple into enchanting scenery. The outside world barely changes yet it is never the same, not for a moment. There are imperceptible changes, barely noticed by the eye yet living proof that stillness exists, the background against which all life is played out.

What happened next was such an imperceptible change. I had been gently prepared for it since my first meditation in the morning; my senses were tuned. At first I was not aware of it at all. It had been no more than an inkling throughout the day, though I was still too absorbed in the phenomena of my observation – of the trees, the grass, the sky – to pay any attention to that which was carrying it all. I observed a rhythmic fractal pattern in the branches, superimposed on the green and absorbed by the branches at the same time. I discerned an underlying symmetry which appeared to be the superstructure holding everything in place rather than the twigs connected to their branches, connected to the trunk, the roots and the earth. As my eyes wandered further afield towards the woods in the distance, there too the fractal rhythms were engaged in the process of holding the world in place. I was astounded that I hadn't noticed this obvious fact before, that reality was sustained and held in place by a super-ordinary rhythm and harmony. No longer did it seem that the trees received their sustenance through their roots, but instead were configured by a powerful super-dimensional aspect of order and harmony, delivered through the air and the stillness surrounding them. This came as a mild surprise to my accustomed way of looking at life, because I now could see with my own eyes that the world was a fabrication of consciousness and my old way of looking at it was just one of many assumptions; and this particular assumption, though not less real, could easily have panned out quite differently.

The same applied to all other objects around me: the wooden boards of my veranda, the ground in front of me, all were subject to a super-dimensional order and intent, primarily not physical at all, but just an outcome, an apparition. Wherever I looked I saw a network of light and energy keeping the air and the objects within it sustained with life and holding it in place.

As I stared at the grass it was the same. The essential aspect of the grass was the light, and the physical blades were just an outcrop of the light. Wherever I looked I found the same, there was nothing more fundamental than the light and it was in, above and surrounding everything without exception, including the thing which I referred to as my body. I noticed with astonishment and without any fuss that I was simply enlightened. There were no ifs or buts. It was just utter simplicity and an indisputable observation of fact. I was stunned that enlightenment could be so natural and without any form of announcement. But what surprised me the most was that I had been enlightened all my life, even for all eternity, but simply had not noticed.

The grass in front of the Sheilin vibrated in light. Around the edges of the patch of grass the light rose into the air as if forming a crown. Wherever I moved my eyes the crown followed, a headdress of light wherever I looked. It showed me that the world was made out of light and there was nothing to dispute the facts or usurp its reality. It was unmistakable and real and seeing it as anything else was just a glitch of perception, a temporary one at that, here one

8 – The Nine-Step Meditation towards Awakening

LIBERATION

Dwelling in wisdom will set me free. I am no longer subjected to pros and cons, to opposites. I simply surrender to the great light of consciousness, because its light is everywhere and because it is everywhere, I am everywhere, no longer attached to anything. I am completely liberated and my home is everywhere. I can feel liberation by letting go. Any problem, any attachment, can teach me liberation the moment I let go and surrender instead to the great light of consciousness, which is simply everywhere in absolute freedom. It has no boundaries.

Because liberation is free I do not tether it or try to grasp it. I simply allow it to be with my attention, allowing it in my awareness, three times.

moment, gone the next, without substance of its own. The light I saw was the true foundation, anything else a mirage. Now I was living in a space where the world showed its true origin in plain sight. All is made of light and I calmly accepted that I was there too and was made of light.

Until now this was just a perceived fact of reality but then I became uncertain. What was the nature of my perception? What perceived it? I felt stranded and turned to my silent companion for support to help me across into the heart of the reality I saw. With the combined strength of my soul and existence I silently shouted through this infinite space of light: 'Convince me, take me to the heart!'

The Ten Minute Moment

I looked over to my left as if I was expecting my own mother to grab my hand and squeeze it reassuringly, but instead a warming wave of love lifted me to my feet and walked me to the opening of the door, where I stared transfixed into the crown of light. I can't determine which caused the ecstasy, the joy that my silent call was responded to by the love of my silent companion which at this moment had proved its reality, or that I found myself standing within a crown of light, being the very light the crown was made of. The only perception was one of an intense ecstasy, where every breath I took fanned its flames and made it more intense. My realisation was not one of knowing but one of being.

Whereas the day before there was an otherness which made me turn and flee, here I had long crossed that point and without any fear. I had already crossed it before I even realised. It had been happening gently all day. And it had been happening all my life and even before I began. I had been enlightened, been the light in my essence, but always forgot. Now, standing in its very centre, the centre of the crown of light, I received its ecstasy. No sign of dread, no otherness, only the realisation of home, irrevocably, my true abode, united with the element that made me.

There are no words to commemorate the vistas of eternal being because words are only a blurry reflection like the lake rippled by the wind. It doesn't touch the land surrounding it. A fish may break the surface of the water, but will plunge back by its own gravity. Had I ceased to be a fish?

For a short while I had breathed the air and seen the surrounding land, basking in ecstasy, in eternity. A brief moment which had shown me what I really was, an enlightened being, not for a single blink divorced from this reality. How foolish to forget.

Words have to be suspended for description, because they would utterly fail, even mislead. All that can be said is that no person on earth can sustain such intensity for long without burning to a cinder or terminating his physical life and entering forever into the ring of fire to be devoured and become one with its own source, at which point all ecstasy must stop.

The moment the ecstasy abated the world came flooding back, and with it all its pain, an ecstatic pain which made me break up into tiny pieces. I began to cry, like a newborn baby seeing the darkness of the daylight for the first time. Every piece of me that shattered was distributed over the whole world, into every atom, feeling its density and pain. In a powerful surge I felt the pain of every living person and I cried out loud, consumed by the suffering of every living creature on this planet. Then I broke down again, consumed by pain yet simultaneously compensated and ravished by an intense ecstasy. Then I was back and yet at the same time still felt strangely yet absolutely connected to my source. I was not abandoned.

After my body had stopped wailing and crying from the pain of its birth and the pain of the world and its disintegration, another part of me stood by my side. It was me, my silent companion. I was the silent companion. I looked with compassion at my body and watched it withering away. The spell had been broken, the illusion destroyed. I was no longer a separate something. I was here to live a new life as somebody I had always been but never realised.

9 – The Nine-Step Meditation towards Awakening

ONENESS

When I find liberation I find oneness. Despite the many forms that exist there is no denying that existence 'is'. Being is and being is everywhere. Being was before the Big Bang, before creation itself. You cannot think without being. There is only one being and I and everything that exists is rooted in being and being is one. At the root of being is oneness, which is the pure light of consciousness, and beyond that is its essence, which is pure being and pure oneness. I simply have to be aware of being and I will reside in oneness. In oneness I enter into the great light of consciousness, outside of which nothing can exist. I simply have to let it be. I am still and open my heart, notice the Oneness and surrender to it.

I am and I am what I am.

I looked at my watch and learned that no more than ten minutes had passed, ten minutes as a fish in the air or as a ravishing flame in an inferno of fire. To endure in this state I would have to cease being a body and become everything instead. I now was again a body, but it was only a veil and that was simply a statement of material fact.

After my ten-minute moment I was still who I was and will be who I am, a man who had regained his memory, endowed with gratitude that he was now aware of the true facts. My origin and my destiny were rolled into one: 'I am nothing and I am everything and nothing will ever change the facts.'

The Ten Minute Moment

Day seven, Thursday, 6 June
Translocating Identity

Contemplation, 4 a.m.

I had no sleep. How could I? I had been in a state of hyper-wakefulness, still observing with curiosity and wonder my shift into a new level of existence. Barely a day ago I had a dream of standing on a tall building, the sky was my ceiling. The tall building was a dream metaphor for myself. I occupied its penthouse suite and from its flat roof I observed, effortlessly, the whole vista surrounding me and the city, and up through the blue canopy of its infinite ceiling I could see all space as if it was my own back yard. This new viewing platform offered an entirely different perspective than from the ground. Looking at my past was like remembering a dream of struggling to climb a big mountain and after resting to recover my strength finding that I was still where I had started, climbing with great effort the immense mountain yet never reaching the top. Now I had become the mountain. My previous life was simply a fantasy, in which I imagined that everything to do with me was of the utmost importance and that it had been my duty to prove to the world that this assumption was justified. How futile this fantasy was.

The only thing from the past that was on offer right now was the fact that the person belonging to it had simply vanished from existence. All this was gone now. I was left standing inside the crown of light which had triggered the event the day before, a ring of light surrounding me which simply gave new meaning to everything I looked at. Although I could no longer see it with the same visual intensity as the day before, I could still sense it, know that it was total certainty and fact. Another powerful feature was that this ring of light, or perhaps this ring of perception, made everything appear as if I was encountering it for the first time, an unbiased new discovery, against which the old ways of looking at things were little more than through a smokescreen. I was the occupier of a completely new entity, which had been liberated from the nebulous ideas which the departed one had taken to be essential.

This new entity had simply evicted the previous occupier from this body and transformed it, had anchored itself within a new superior reality, where everything was sharper, more clearly defined and cleared of any of the old deceptions, like the idea that my physical body was central to my identity. This body now had a new rightful owner who no longer had such a limited viewpoint. It no longer saw positives or negatives, only different perspectives. Instead of viewpoints it saw different states of being. A new clarity informed it that there was neither an outside nor an inside, neither a me nor an otherness. It was inconceivable to think of the world in terms of such duality. It simply could no longer find a foothold in such crude understandings of reality.

No matter what I did or thought of I could only ever be in this one place, which was not and could not be separated from anything at all. Wherever I looked, whatever caught my attention was simply an integral part of who I was, which meant as much to me as my own body. There was no going back. I had entered the core reality of all things, broken the spell of the illusion of being separate from an outside world. I no longer stood apart or was able to act as if I was divorced from the world or from what I perceived. I had stopped being in a time and a place and had become a field which no longer had a limiting horizon. This field had no beginning and no end either, and was created and recreated anew every moment. I felt equally attracted to any object entering my field no matter what state it represented to the world. I saw a flower as the essential flower, whether it was just a seed, a seedling, a bud, in full bloom or withering away and falling from its stem. Its essential flowerness was still apparent, even as it lay in the mud.

I no longer had to concern myself about how to function in this vast and ever-new field of unity which displayed zillions of forms with endless opportunities to grow and to explore. I could act, speak and think in accordance with what was, without having to worry in the least that I was doing the right thing. I could rely on the authenticity of my thoughts as they emerged unfiltered and free of judgements from a deep and pure, unprejudiced origin which already knew and understood all things. A new authority emerged, gently yet firmly asserting its control, authorised by being directly connected to what was true and authentic. It needed no persuasion and simply acted from a source of intrinsic wisdom. It simply did what was needed to be done to evolve its inner nature without needing to ask questions or search for answers. Stillness and the clear light of consciousness were all around me and I had instant access.

There was no longer a good or bad, just the impartial essence of everything. No longer did I need to separate things from one another in order to sort them into a system of values, decide which was good and which was better, which was worthy and which unworthy. I simply accepted the roles, the assignments and functions of the world as an integral part of its existence. Wherever I looked all I could see was existence in progress, manifestation in its own right rooted in one being, there for a purpose which had its assigned place in this world, to evolve, to learn and to unfold.

Would it last or was this simply a transient abode, a temporary escape from the shackles of mortal life? Can such realisation be maintained? Is it at all possible to survive in a world stripped of its traditional values and allocated meanings? How could such a world be maintained in a human environment which is largely judged by appearances? Maintaining it would need a maintainer, but with everything else the maintainer had left. I quickly realised that maintenance took care of itself and that my life from now on would be a continuous process of letting go and rejoicing in the fact that there could be nothing of which I was not already an integral part of.

Something was permanently broken, like a cage of frosted glass, which had shattered into millions of pieces and was now allowing me to breathe the fresh air and see the world clearly as if for the first time. It would need a miracle and superhuman effort to fit all these tiny pieces of glass back into a frosted-glass cage.

Yes, I had known stillness before, a daily blessing handed to me by my silent companion, who reminded me of it the moment I opened my eyes. Where was my silent companion now? It was right here, within me, right next to me and in front of me. It was in my hands and body and I could see the world through its eyes. By having become its equal I had become it. I was the silent companion. It was my heart, my blood and my perception. I saw what it had seen all my life while I was still half asleep, mistaking my dream for reality. Now I could see what it saw all along. I understood why it was silent and resting in the deeper knowledge that was now laid out before me. In the past it had pointed me to the truth when I asked for it and now I simply shared it from its position and viewpoint; all I had to do now was simply open my eyes and look and see. And as I looked and saw, a warm thrill and benediction washed over me to confirm that it was the truth.

I had a cup of coffee and accidentally doubled the dose. I had taken an extra sachet from my tea tray at the last bed-and-breakfast place on my way here to my retreat, thinking it was sugar. I had prejudged that Buddhist devotees would frown upon such unhealthy indulgences as sugar, an attitude which was unfounded of course – even some hermits take sugar. So instead of sugar I now had a double-strength coffee, perhaps teaching me 'though shalt not steal'. On the positive side it had an invigorating effect, making me even more alert to my new senses. Back then, which was barely a week ago, I would only have relied reluctantly on my instinct.

With my mind awake and clear it was time to meditate. Looking through my open door and breathing the crisp air I found that the morning fog had erased the mountain beyond the first line of trees. I saw a number of cobwebs in the grass at regular intervals. They were clearly defined, having caught the morning dew. They glistened and glowed in the first twilight, creating their own tapestry of pattern in the grass. The birds were already at it, spinning their colourful fractal melodies and reassuring me that I had acquired an extra layer of appreciation.

Despite not having slept, I felt refreshed, not tired at all, and I am sure it wasn't just the coffee. I very much felt the tranquil joy carried over from the previous day. I could not fix it in any place. It

The Ten Minute Moment

was in the air as well as in my body and as I focused on the mist I felt it there too as if I was the mist. When I listened to the stream in the gorge a few hundred yards to my right its joy was carried to my ears. Everywhere was the placid reassurance of stillness which confirmed that I had been translocated into a permanent new state of consciousness. All the atoms in my body had been ignited in the process and retuned as new and additional organs of perception. I could see and hear with my skin and the air too filling my space became a means by which I perceived.

I filled the kettle to make tea, the splattering tune of the water and the closing thud of the lid completing a short sound score. I dwelled in a song of love. Yes, love was everywhere, wherever I turned. Everything my hands touched had a serene familiarity and all felt purposeful and right. The chaos of my clothes thrown thoughtlessly over the chair the previous night and hanging limply over the back displayed a distinct note of humour, as did the sorry heap of the rest of my clothes on the floor. The untidiness of my table, where I had casually swept everything to one side with one arm-stroke in order to make room to write, it too looked charmingly attractive. My camera, hoods, tissue paper and random bits and pieces created a theatre piece of visual performance in which each object had a meaning, an assigned part to play, an existence to fill and a comment to make. I felt tender affection for each of these modest actors.

Everything I turned my eyes to spoke to me, all had a purpose and each was the centre of its world, ensouled by stillness and meaning. Stillness had taken possession of my hut. I had been assimilated by it and now I understood that not a single item was out of place.

I finally merged into my beanbag and, looking through the open door, I settled down into my meditation. There was no hurry, no plan. I was already meditating and wherever I would go from here I would be residing in stillness meditation. I considered going out and taking photos but, for this moment at least, there was no need. The place and the moment I was in was good then and the moment I am in now as I write these words – and as anybody reading them will realise – is the same moment and the only moment that exists.

THE END

Epilogue
Twelve Markers of an Awakened Life

How does a profound shift in consciousness affect daily life? I found at least twelve major changes which made my new identity different from the old one:

1. Ecstatic Joy

There is an underlying feeling of ecstatic joy in life from the moment I wake up. There is an increase of spontaneous peak experiences during the day.

2. Feeling of 'Home'

I have an ongoing feeling that I am on 'home ground' no matter where I am. The world is a familiar place with a constant feeling of being 'home'. It feel as if the inside and the outside world are no longer separate places, but have merged into one.

3. Detachment

I no longer feel identified with personal comments or criticism directed at me, but it doesn't mean I am indifferent. Praise and insult don't reach very deep and mean very little.

4. Enhanced Empathy

I feel strong empathy with other living things, not just people and animals, but with life general. I feel engagement with the world without getting attached to it.

5. Living in the Moment

I feel an acute awareness of the present moment and perceive it as new and unique. This living awareness of reality takes precedence over all thoughts or concepts.

6. No Experience of Repetition or Boredom

I do not experience any feelings of repetition despite routines. Every moment is new and experienced as if for the first time. There is no room for boredom.

7. Thoughts are viewed at a Distance

Thoughts are mostly detached and viewed at a distance without holding any power over me. I can pick them and let them go with equal ease.

8. Living through the Heart

The heart assesses situations instantly and intuitively from an inner wisdom level instead of employing linear brainwork thinking with its endless pros and cons. Obviously the brain is still employed as a tool and an instrument.

9. Enhanced Sensual Awareness

My perception is largely channelled via the heart leading to strong engagement with the world and other people. Feelings and passions arising out of challenging situations settle down quickly without leaving any residue.

10. Peace and Inner Security

I am constantly aware of peace and stillness which can be experienced as a kind of presence, of not being alone or perhaps an awareness of residing inside a greater space of intelligence or consciousness.

11. No Fear of Death

Death is no longer seen as the end because life is perceived as an infinite and continuously unfolding process without boundaries, although this doesn't affect the instinct for survival.

12. Unlimited Freedom

Because experiences are no longer related to limited ego or social identification, life is experienced in a state of total freedom and individual sovereignty. It offers vast opportunities with a powerful potential for growth.

The Nine Step Meditation to Oneness

This combines the Nine Step Meditation into one. It should be practiced with light and ease and without effort or concentration. This technique is most effective if conducted almost passively, as a kind of 'noticing' and allowing oneself to be drawn into it instead of using 'intent'. Consciousness is at its most effective if it is not interfered with, and allowing oneself to be absorbed by it. Each word is the subject of the meditation. Each word is observed in the space of consciousness before me, picked up with an attitude of gratefulness. I then allow the word to take ownership of me, still in gratitude. I simply observe or notice where it takes me, without thought, just with the feeling in my heart. Gratitude is the key, because it puts me into a position of humility, which is needed in order to surrender to each word.

The first word is LOVE

I simply observe LOVE rising from the heart. If I cannot feel it at first, I find gratitude. There is always something to be grateful for in my life. Once I notice gratitude, I observe that love is at its heart. Then I surrender to love. If thoughts begin to interfere, I simply let it go without attachment and pick up the next word.

The second word is RADIANCE

I feel the radiance of Love and how it radiates its power out into all space around me. Radiance is light and easy. I simply allow myself to be carried out into the infinite space of consciousness, via radiance, and only do so as long as it lasts, even if it is only for a few seconds and then I let it go of its own accord.

The third word is UNITY

I simply allow Consciousness to reveal UNITY to me. Observing the word, as I would observe a butterfly, without interference. I pick up each word gently three times and allow it to float through my awareness. After I have observed LOVE and RADIANCE I observe it leading me to UNION and UNITY.

The fourth word is WELL BEING

Lightly and naturally I observe the 'feeling tone' of these manifestations within my being and hand it to my attention a few times and then attend to the next word. From UNITY WELL BEING and Health arise and I 'reside' in this awareness. I feel it naturally inside me until it withdraws or thought intrudes and then I let it go to give rise to STRENGTH.

The fifth word is STRENGTH

STRENGTH is naturally released through WELL BEING and I let STRENGTH carry me, guide me naturally and allow it to spread into every aspect of my awareness. There is no part in me which is not touched by STRENGTH. It invigorates my whole being and soul until it naturally fades when I let it go when I allow ABUNDANCE to arise.

The sixth word is ABUNDANCE

All inner and outer space is filled with ABUNDANCE. ABUNDANCE which is everywhere and there can be no shortfall because the whole universe exists because of ABUNDANCE and out of ABUNDANCE rises abundant WISDOM.

The seventh word is WISDOM

ABUNDANCE is guided by WISDOM and WISDOM underpins all of creation and all of nature. I feel WISDOM in my heart and observe how it guides all my steps in life, all my thoughts and decisions. I simply have to surrender to its deep cosmic intelligence and trust it with my heart

The eighth word is LIBERATION

This Wisdom 'attitude' sets me free and leads to me to LIBERATION, which shows me I am an unlimited being with infinite potential. I rest in the word as long as it allows me to and then let it go. LIBERATION transcends all limitations and will result in ONENESS and enlightenment.

The Ten Minute Moment

The ninth word is ONENESS

The last word I reside in is ONENESS, the total surrender to my essence. I absolutely surrender to the essence of my own being. I return to my home, my origins, into the ocean of all consciousness in absolute joy, freedom, stillness and peace and I can remember where I belong any and every time I choose during my waking day.

None of this requires any effort, only an open-mindedness which allows the light of consciousness to reveal the inner meanings of these words. I let the light of consciousness guide my meditation. I have no part in it other than to surrender. Surrendering unfolds all these steps before me naturally without my seeking it. The light of consciousness is the true carrier of these words. I simply surrender to these words and become aware of the light of consciousness carrying them.
This is the short way I have found to LIBERATION and ONENESS. I do not have to sit long in this meditation just as the light of consciousness allows it even if it is only for a few seconds. I don't meditate. I am meditated by CONSCIOUSNESS and by settling lightly on each word. I let it reside in my awareness and then let it be. ONENESS comes to me. I do not seek oneness. I simply allow it to be.

This is the meditation of ONENESS.
I am.

For more information please visit the author's websites:
www.thetenminutemoment.com - www.multidimensionalman.com

Printed in Great Britain
by Amazon